A GUIDE TO
BASE

ANDREW THOMAS

Macdonald
Queen Anne Press

A *Queen Anne Press* BOOK

© by Andrew Thomas 1986

First published in Great Britain in 1986 by
Queen Anne Press, a division of
Macdonald & Co (Publishers) Ltd
Greater London House, London NW1 7QX

A BPCC plc Company
Reprinted 1987

ISBN 0 356 12743 5

Typeset by Bookworm Typesetting, Manchester.
Printed and bound in Great Britain by R. J. Acford, Chichester.

CONTENTS

INTRODUCTION 6

1. **BASEBALL and ROUNDERS** 8

2. **THE PLAYING FIELD** 11
Home Plate 11
The Bases 14
The Pitcher's Mound and Plate 15
The Positions of Fielders and Officials 17

3. **BASEBALL EQUIPMENT** 18
The Bat 18
The Ball 20
Baseball Clothing and Uniforms 21
Fielding Gloves 25
The Catcher's Equipment 26

4. **PLAYING SKILLS** 29
Fitness and Practice 29
The Pitcher 30
The Catcher 39
Infielders 43
Outfielders 52
The Batter 55
Game Situations 67
The Umpires 73
The Manager and Coaches 76

5. **MAJOR LEAGUE BASEBALL** 78
Following Major League Baseball in Britain 81
Scoring a Baseball Game 82

6. **BASEBALL AROUND THE WORLD** 86

7. **BASEBALL IN BRITAIN** 91

8. **BASEBALL RULES AND TERMS** 94

9. **USEFUL ADDRESSES** 102

INTRODUCTION

Britain's appetite for things American has developed a stage beyond chewing gum, credit cards and fast food. In the last few years, thanks to television's influence on cultural activities in Britain and other European countries, and increasing travel across the Atlantic, American sports have made a massive impact, and one that is still growing.

The most spectacular example is American football. The professionals of the NFL now have millions of armchair fans from Newcastle to Naples, while other winter sports such as ice-hockey and basketball, long time favourites in certain areas of Britain, have made similar huge advances here and on the continent.

Baseball, a summer sport and by tradition America's national pastime, has at least one great advantage over the other games mentioned. Although at the highest level the players are skilful gifted athletes supplied with expensive and scientifically designed specialised equipment, almost anyone can join in and enjoy an impromptu game of baseball in the park or playground, or on the beach. All that is needed is something to mark the bases, a bat, and a ball (a soft rubber baseball or even a tennis ball will do).

It is a popular assumption that, although baseball is played throughout the world, it is as American as Coca Cola or mom's apple pie. Indeed, the Spalding Commission was formed in the early years of this century, with the intention of declaring baseball a wholly American invention. It was not until just before the Second World War, when a New York librarian, R.W. Henderson, published irrefutable evidence about the game's origins, that Americans were

A GUIDE TO
BASEBALL

forced to accept that baseball had evolved from pastimes such as rounders, stoolball and cricket. These games had been taken to North America by migrants from various parts of the British Isles during the seventeenth and eighteenth centuries. It was during the nineteenth century that Americans developed baseball to its present state and made it peculiarly their own.

To many it is surprise enough that baseball is played in this country at all, let alone to discover that the earliest baseball association in Britain was formed in 1890. The sport was particularly popular with working people in London, the Midlands and North of England where many baseball clubs developed in association with soccer teams such as Nottingham Forest and Tottenham Hotspur. Indeed the home ground of Derby County F.C. is still called the Baseball Ground. Baseball reached a peak here during the 1930s when many thousands would attend the big games, and in 1938 Britain won baseball's first amateur world championship.

With so many Americans stationed in Britain during the Second World War baseball might have been expected to go from strength to strength. However, although baseball continued to be played in a few parts of the country in the post-war years, it is only recently that enthusiasm for the sport has revived. But the revival has been startling. The number of clubs affiliated to the British Amateur Baseball and Softball Federation has risen rapidly to over 70, while ever increasing numbers are playing social games during the summer in local parks and on playing fields.

This guide, written specifically for the British player and fan, makes regular reference to the exceptional skills of those who play professional major league baseball in North America. As these top players are the ones most likely to be read about or seen on television, their achievements are used to illustrate the game as played at the highest level. In addition, the many hints and suggestions for beginners should prove helpful for the growing numbers of those keen to start playing baseball, besides providing background information for fans content to enjoy the sport on radio and television, or watch friends playing baseball in the park.

CHAPTER ONE

BASEBALL AND ROUNDERS

Many people will have played rounders, probably at school. As rounders has obvious features in common with baseball it will be useful to illustrate broad similarities and differences between the two games.

Baseball, like rounders, is a game between two teams of nine players in which each team takes turns at batting and tries to score more runs than the other. However, a cursory glance at the dimensions labelled on Figs 1 and 2 opposite, comparing the two games, soon shows the differences in scale and power involved.

With some exceptions, in baseball a team scores a run each time one of its players completes a circuit of the square, which is termed the diamond. In rounders, a player must complete the whole circuit before the next ball is bowled in order to score one run, but in baseball a run is scored each time a player arrives at home plate without being put out, whether or not he has stopped at bases.

Three corners of the square are marked by fixed, flat, bases, 15 inches square, instead of the 4-foot posts used in rounders. The remaining corner is the home plate, a five-sided piece of white rubber, 17 inches wide. The batter stands beside home plate in a batter's box ready to receive the leather-covered cork ball from the pitcher. All nine players take turns to bat. When only three of the batting side have been put out, the other team gets a turn to bat until three of its players are out. When both teams have batted it is called an inning. While there are two innings a side in most rounders games, there are usually nine innings in a game of baseball, which lasts for about three hours in the North American major leagues. When one team is batting the other team is fielding, and the fielders try to stop the batters scoring runs. A pitcher on the fielding team stands on the pitcher's mound in the centre of the diamond and throws the white ball, which is about the same size

Fig 1. The Baseball Diamond

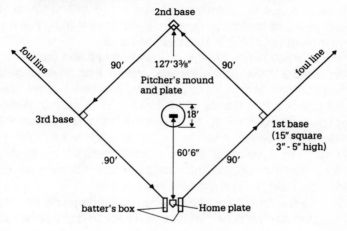

Fig 2. The Rounders Pitch

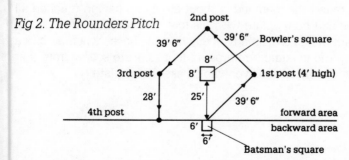

and weight as a cricket ball. Unlike a bowler in rounders, the pitcher does not have to release the ball underarm, but may throw it side-arm or over-arm as hard or softly as he wishes towards home plate.

The batter stands next to home plate holding a bat up to three and a half feet long (more than twice the length of a rounders bat) with both hands. If he hits the ball in the area between the two foul lines in the permitted way, he has to run towards the first base. Unlike the batter in rounders, a baseball batter does not have a choice of balls on which to run. However, he cannot run if the ball is hit outside the 90-degree arc between the left and right foul lines, whereas in rounders, a batter may run if the ball is hit in the 180-degree arc of the forward area or go to 1st post if the ball is hit safely (without bouncing) in the backward area.

If the baseball batter swings at a pitched ball and misses, it is usually called a 'strike'. It is also called a strike if he does not swing at a ball that passes over home plate between the top of his knees and his arm pits (not the top of his head as in rounders). When a batter has received three strikes he is out. A pitch outside the strike zone described, which is not swung at, is called a 'ball'. When a batter receives four 'balls' he is given a walk to 1st base. In rounders, after three consecutive balls the batter is awarded a ½ rounder, but this rule does not exist in baseball.

When he has hit the ball the baseball batter drops his bat, then runs to 1st base, 2nd base, 3rd base and back to home plate in an anti-clockwise direction to score a run. If a player is able to run all the way round the diamond without stopping, having touched all the bases and home plate with his foot it is called a home run. If three team mates are already occupying the bases when he hits a home run, the maximum number of four runs are scored from that single hit, one by each player who crosses home plate.

CHAPTER TWO

THE
PLAYING FIELD

Figs 3 & 4 overleaf show detailed markings of the batter's boxes and catcher's box around home plate, and the general markings and measurements across the infield to include the arc 95 feet from the centre of the pitcher's mound.

For a new spectator, the eye would be drawn to the presence of the pitcher's mound, and the way the three white bases and home plate stand out sharply against the sandy soil of the infield base paths and the mown grass or artificial turf of the infield and outfield.

It is a surprise for many to find out how much closer to the action one may sit than at most ball games. The duel between bowler and batsman on a cricket pitch usually takes place more than 60 yards from the boundary rope. But, because the action on a baseball field takes place within the 90-degree arc of fair territory and its immediate fringe, it is possible to sit much closer to the play. One may become aware of the nuances of the contest between batter and pitcher, or involved in the plays around the foul lines or the dugouts, which are sometimes too close for comfort. The wide open space of the outfield is large enough to contain an international-size soccer pitch, provided the pitcher's mound is levelled and the various fixtures and fittings removed! In fact England scored a memorable 3-2 victory over Italy in Yankee Stadium, New York in May 1976.

Since the first full-size indoor stadium, the Houston Astrodome, was built in the mid-1960s, several stadia in North America have replaced their grass with a carpet of bright-green Astro-Turf 8 which has a concrete underlay. Two other indoor stadia are used by major league-teams, in Seattle and Minneapolis, while a further eight clubs now play their home games on Astro-Turf.

There is no doubt that baseball has to be played differently on artificial turf, with its considerably faster surface. For example, outfielders, for instance, must be able to run particularly fast to gather the skidding ball, but they do not need such a strong arm as on grass. A bouncing throw will race on through an Astro-Turf infield to 3rd base or home plate reducing the need for a relay throw from the 2nd baseman or shortstop. Batters take advantage of the

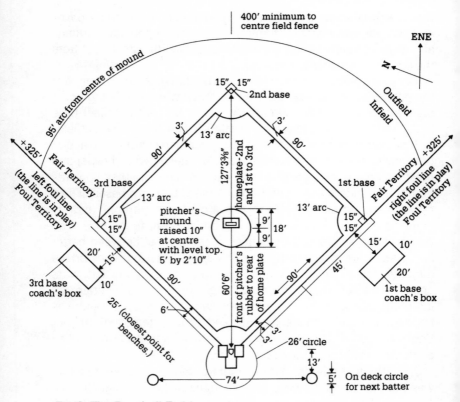

*Fig 3. The Baseball Field,
featuring the infield markings*

higher bounce from the artificial surface by chop-hitting the ball down into the ground rather than risk being caught out. They are less likely to bunt (to hit the ball gently a few yards into the infield) as the unyielding surface sends the ball skidding away too fast.

In Britain baseball is played on grass. Very few clubs have their own diamonds and most play on multi-use playing fields or parks without the luxury of infield base paths, concrete anchors for the three bases set below ground level, or even a raised pitcher's mound. Once the appropriate white lines have been marked, home plate and the pitcher's rubber are held in place with screw-in spikes, while the three bases are secured by long metal hooks like tent pegs, which are hammered or tamped into the turf. It would seem a prudent investment for a club with limited funds to borrow or purchase five or six lengths (about 25 yards) of nylon netting with supporting poles, ropes and pegs. If these nets are put up before each game in an arc 60 feet behind home plate, and parallel with the two foul lines, they prove a valuable aid to player and spectator safety. Although a number of top edges will go high over such netting it will catch many balls snicked behind home plate and avoid a great deal of wasted time spent running back to collect missed or wild pitches. Clubs with a more secure home ground would obviously be able to construct more permanent facilities.

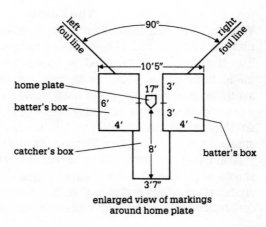

Fig 4. Details of markings around home plate

enlarged view of markings around home plate

13

Home Plate

This is a five-sided piece of white rubber next to which the batter stands, and over which the pitcher attempts to pitch the ball. It is supplied with screw-in spikes to fix the 20lb plate to the ground at the junction of the left and right foul lines. Home plate is in fair territory with its point exactly 60 feet 6 inches from the front edge of the pitcher's rubber on the mound; it has bevelled edges to reduce the risk of injury to base runners as they slide in an attempt to score a run. *(See Fig 5.)*

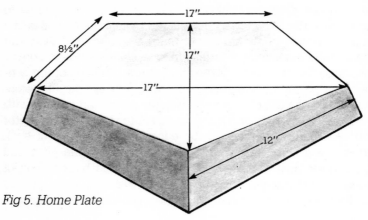

Fig 5. Home Plate

The Bases

When a batter hits the ball correctly he attempts to run from home plate to 1st base, to 2nd base, to 3rd base and back to home plate. The three white bases used in baseball have traditionally been made from canvas, filled with soft padding, but longer-lasting synthetic materials are often used nowadays. Some of baseball's more spectacular and rugged action takes place around the bases, so they must be strong enough to withstand the impact of sprawling players and their flying studs and cleats.

The bases are anchored to the ground. This may be with metal spikes and tapes (for the cheaper bases used in parks), or by an anchor plate which is attached to the underside of the base and to a concrete weight set several inches below ground level. 1st and 3rd

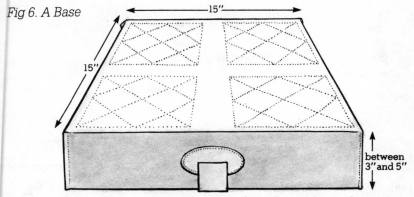

Fig 6. A Base

15″

15″

between 3″ and 5″

base must be fixed inside the foul lines (which are themselves in play), while the middle of 2nd base is set on the point where the lines from 1st and 3rd base meet. The bases must be easily removable, as the ground crew may have to replace or rotate the bags and repair damage to the infield. *(See Fig 6.)*

The Pitcher's Mound and Plate

The pitcher's mound must be 10 inches high and have a flat top, from which it should slope down to the edges of the circle.

The pitcher's rubber is set with its long axis parallel to the front edge of the home plate. The pitcher's plate in the majors is a square piece of white rubber with a reinforced aluminium tube like a relay baton down its centre. In many leagues the pitcher's rubber is a flattened rectangle, with three screw-in spikes to fix the rubber to the mound. *(See Fig 7.)*

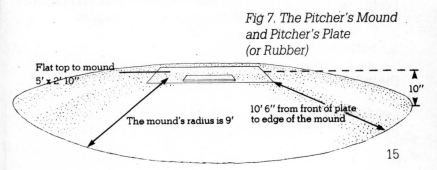

Fig 7. The Pitcher's Mound and Pitcher's Plate (or Rubber)

Flat top to mound 5′ x 2′ 10″

10″

The mound's radius is 9′

10′ 6″ from front of plate to edge of the mound

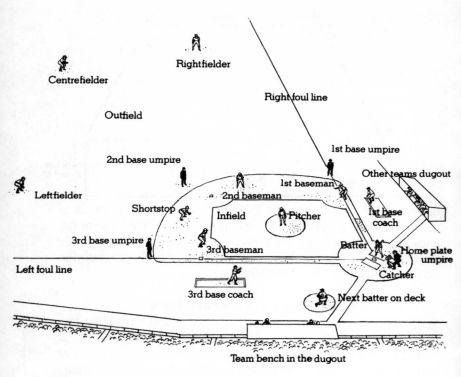

Fig 8. Positions of players and game officials

The Positions of Fielders and Officials

Fig 8 shows the nine fielders (and the batter) on the field labelled with abbreviations for each of the usual fielding positions.

The **battery** is the pitcher	(p)
and the catcher	(c)
The **infield** is made up of the 1st baseman	(1b)
and the 2nd baseman	(2b)
and the 3rd baseman	(3b)
and the shortstop	(ss)

Although the shortstop tends to field between the 2nd and 3rd basemen he may change his position in the field more than the others depending on the situation of the game and the hitter at bat.

The **outfield** is made up of the leftfielder (lf)
and the centrefielder (cf)
and the rightfielder (rf)

The outfielders are named from the batter's point of view, looking out at the field. The bat boys are lads of high school age who keep the bats and other dugout equipment neat and tidy at home games.

CHAPTER THREE

BASEBALL EQUIPMENT

The international nature of baseball in the 1980s is reflected in the variety of countries that produce playing equipment for their own and overseas markets. Even in the USA, most gloves, shoes, and protective equipment are made in Japan, Korea or Taiwan, while official major league baseballs are made in Haiti.

The Bat

A baseball bat is a smooth, rounded stick, longer than a cricket bat but not as wide. Many years ago bats were made of hard, heavy hickory, but these days wooden bats are made from northern white ash grown in New York State and Pennsylvania. About 200,000 50-year-old trees are cut down each year by the major bat-making companies, and the wood from trees is air dried for about eight months before being shaped on a lathe. Each tree has enough wood for about 50 bats, of which five will be good enough for major league players and the remainder for retail.

Major league players must use wooden bats, but eight out of ten bats sold these days are made of aluminium. Although more expensive these last far longer than a wooden bat. *(See Fig 9.)* Major leaguers use 70 or so bats in a season, and each is made to their exact specifications. These may reflect their personal hitting preferences, have characteristics to suit particular pitchers or particular ball parks, or merely conform to the latest fashion. Some want natural wood, flame-tempered wood, painted black, two-tone, or rubbed with a bottle or bones to close the pores and strengthen the wood. Major league bats weigh between 2 and 2½ lbs, and few use bats as heavy as the 2lbs 11ozs clubs swung by Lou Gehrig in the 1930s. Most bats are between 2 feet 6 inches and 3 feet in length. Each has a 'sweet spot' which is about 8 or 10 inches from its end, and from which the ball appears to leap away without much effort. There is an old wives' tale that if the ball hits the writing on the bat then the bat will break.

To improve their grip, players may wear a light batting glove or rub a pine tar rag on the top 18 inches of the handle. They must be careful not to let it spread too far. In 1983 George Brett (Kansas City) had a home run against the Yankees disallowed for too much pine tar down the bat. On appeal the homer was counted the next day, the suspended game completed, and the rules quickly changed to avoid a recurrence of the problem.

To speed the snap of their swing some players practise immediately before stepping up to bat with two bats, or slip a bat weight or 'doughnut' on the barrel. When it is taken off, the bat seems that much easier to handle.

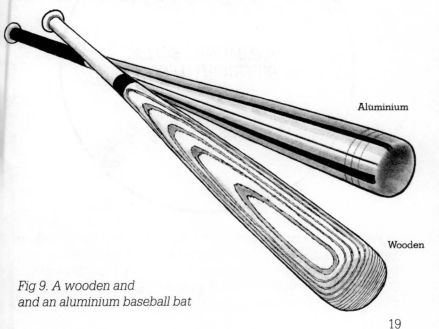

Aluminium

Wooden

Fig 9. A wooden and and an aluminium baseball bat

The Ball

In 1872 the size and weight of a baseball was standardised as slightly smaller and slightly lighter than a cricket ball, which had been standardised 30 years previously. Making baseballs is a skilled, labour-intensive industry; most are made in Haiti in an eight stage process. The hard ball starts with a soft cork centre covered with two layers of rubber, then three layers of grey and white wool yarn, a layer of fine cotton, and glue to fix the whitened cowhide cover. This has 108 red double stitches in the same pattern as on a tennis ball. The ball is then rolled in a machine to flatten the seams, and finally stamped appropriately.

Fig 10. A baseball

For over 30 years both the National League and the American League have bought Lena Blackburn's Rubbing Mud. This is used by umpires to take the shine off the ball before it is used in a game. The fine abrasive mud, which does not damage or mark the ball, is found in the tidal reaches of the Delaware River near Palmyra, New

Jersey, although the exact location is a secret.

In Japan, the traditional baseball was considered too hard for young boys and girls, and those who played for their own enjoyment, so in 1919 Suzuka Sakae invented a soft, hollow, rubber baseball. This excellent innovation became extremely popular. The modern Nagase ball is used by about 10 million children and adults in Japan, while the official Amateur Rubber Ball Baseball Association has over 70,000 registered teams.

There is a natural reluctance with young players and beginners everywhere to catch a strongly hit hard ball, even when wearing a fielder's glove. Consequently, as in cricket, there seems little wrong with beginners using the Japanese rubber ball, or a soft baseball, or even a tennis ball. West Indian youngsters learn their cricket with a soft ball, and no one would suggest that this has hampered their development.

Baseball clothing

Baseball players throughout the world wear a distinctive uniform characterised by the short-legged trousers, stirrup stockings, and baseball cap.

The baseball cap seems to have become almost universal headgear in recent years. Caps may be in wool or synthetic fibre and of various designs, weights, and prices. Many fans favour the adjustable one-size-fits-all design with the official club logo above the peak. Players are rarely seen without a cap on their head; they wear one when fielding, under their batting helmet when at bat, and running the bases. Major league clubs go through several thousand caps a season, many of which are sold to or stolen by fans.

Helmets did not become compulsory for batters and base runners in the major leagues until 1971 (30 years after they were first worn). Modern helmets are made of smooth, glossy, moulded plastic called Cycolac and are designed to deflect the impact of a pitched ball. A batting helmet must now have at least one ear flap and may have two. It should not be used if cracked or otherwise damaged.

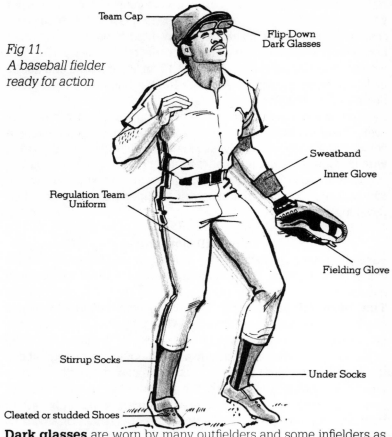

Fig 11.
A baseball fielder
ready for action

Team Cap

Flip-Down
Dark Glasses

Sweatband

Inner Glove

Regulation Team
Uniform

Fielding Glove

Stirrup Socks

Under Socks

Cleated or studded Shoes

Dark glasses are worn by many outfielders and some infielders as they are invaluable when looking up into the sun or stadium lights for high fly balls. Most wear plastic, flip-up glasses with a hinge, so that the fielder has the choice whether to have the 'shades' up or down.

Batting gloves are now worn on one or both hands by many players, much to the disgust of the old timers. Unlike cricket batting gloves, those used in baseball offer little or no protection from a pitched ball, being more like golf gloves. Some players wear a batting glove inside their fielding glove, while others say they prefer not to, as they consider the inner glove reduces their control of the glove.

Uniforms

Baseball players are used to playing in weather conditions which may vary between the chilly damp of San Francisco and the icy winds of Montreal in April, or the heat of Texas in August. So, depending on the weather and personal preferences, players may wear a 'T' shirt, vest, or sweatshirt beneath their uniforms. They will also wear pants and a jockstrap with protective cup; many tape their ankles before putting on their white cotton socks and the characteristic stirrup stockings. The uniform trousers and shirts are no longer the baggy heavy items players had to wear before synthetic double-knit nylon polyester. The modern fashion is for particularly close fitting uniforms. *(See Fig 11.)* Uniforms are in club colours with logos on the chest and perhaps the arms. Each player has his squad number six inches tall on his back, and smaller numbers on the chest. Official surnames may be attached above the numbers on their back, but no advertisements are permitted on clothing in the major leagues. For over 70 years the home team has worn a white-based uniform, while the away team wears grey or coloured shirts and trousers. In the majors, clubs tend to print the team's nickname across the chest of their home uniforms, but name the club's home city instead, for games played 'on the road'. Players also wear a padded 'warm-up' jacket before the game or while sitting on the bench.

The classic baseball uniforms in the majors are worn by the Los Angeles Dodgers in 'Dodger Blue', and the pinstripes of the New York Yankees.

Baseball shoes have traditionally been made of kangaroo hide, stained black. The modern multi-coloured nylon shoes are extremely light and seem designed for track runners rather than base runners. The moulded soles may have blunt steel cleats for turf

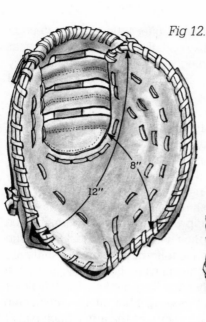

Fig 12. A 1st baseman's mitt

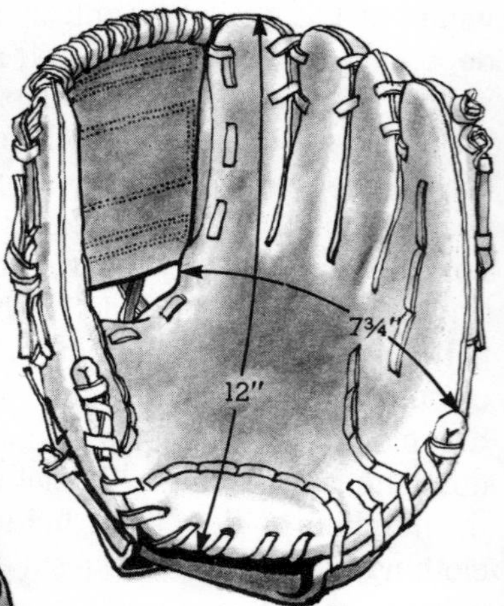

Fig 13. An infielder's glove

The dense webbing helps hide the ball from the batter.

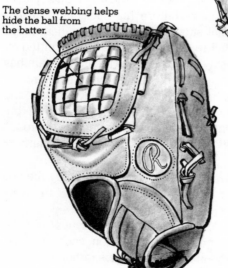

Fig 14. A pitcher's glove

fields or multi-studded rubber for artificial surfaces, but players are not allowed to have pointed spikes like those for golf or athletics. A recently developed shoe worn by two great base runners, Pete Rose and Rickey Henderson, has cleats angled backwards.

The pitcher's shoe on his pivot foot (the one in contact with the pitcher's rubber) has a toe cap to protect his foot.

Fielding Gloves

To a cricketer or rounders player watching baseball on TV, the sight of a baseballer wearing a glove or mitt on the non-throwing hand seems strange. But it does not take long when watching in the ball park to realise that to catch and relay the ball, hit or thrown as hard as it is, without a glove would be risking severe injury to the hand. Even so the use of a glove for fielding is not compulsory.

The first gloves were worn in baseball in the 1870s (about 50 years after cricket wicket-keepers started to wear gloves). Webbing was soon allowed between the thumb and index finger but gloves did not develop much more until after the First World War, when they certainly started to help reduce the number of fielding errors. Modern gloves are made of brown cowhide or synthetic materials in a range of colours, while each position has its specially designed glove or mitt, with official limits to its size.

The 1st baseman's mitt *(See Fig 12)* is larger than the gloves worn by other fielders. It has extra webbing to help pouch the ball. The other three infielders tend to use smaller gloves *(See Fig 13)* with a loop of leather inside to allow the glove to be worn more loosely on the hand. Outfielders may use a glove with a deep pocket (to help gather deep fly balls and line drive), which is not quite as wide as the 1st baseman's mitt. A pitcher may use a glove the same size as an outfielder but it will have extra webbing to help hide the pitcher's grip on the ball, and it may not be multi-coloured, grey or white in case it distracts the batter. *(See Fig 14.)* Major leaguers look after their fielding gloves by rubbing vegetable oil into them to help keep the leather supple. Some players will not allow anyone else to wear their fielding glove, or the other gloves they may spend several years 'breaking in'.

The Catcher's Equipment

The remaining member of the fielding side, the catcher, cannot play effectively unless he is wearing protective clothing. *(See Fig 15.)* These are sometimes called his 'Tools of Ignorance', implying that a catcher must be a little crazy to play in such a potentially hazardous position on the field. Houston pitcher Nolan Ryan's fastball has been timed at 100.9 mph, yet the catcher, just over 20 yards away, would be expected to gather in any pitches the batter did not hit. It is rather like a wicketkeeper being expected to stand up to the wicket to take Malcolm Marshall's fast bowling.

A catcher usually wears a batting helmet back to front under his face mask. This mask has foam padding, steel and wire bars, and a throat protector, and is held on the head with elastic straps which makes it easier to throw away when the catcher goes to field any balls hit near home plate, or runs to cover 1st base. On his chest the catcher will wear a protector of padded canvas or plastic, fastened by a harness, and below it, an abdominal protector and cup.

As he works from a crouched or squatting position, thigh protection is not needed, but knee-, shin-, ankle- and foot-guards are important. The catcher's mitt once resembled a mis-shapen brown pillow, but in 1965 its size was limited. Nowadays there are much lighter and smaller leather mitts, some with Sorbothane which absorbs much of the impact of a fast, hard-pitched ball.

Despite all the protective clothing, this is not a position for the frail or timid. The catcher is still the most likely player in baseball to be injured. He may suffer muscle strain in his back, or legs through not warming up properly before the game; but the most common problems are impact injuries, such as when a pitch is deflected by the batter into thinner parts of the padding (e.g. above and below the knees), or where protection is absent (e.g. the arms or bare hand). As if this were not enough, catchers may also be injured when attempting to put out a base runner who is sliding feet-first towards home plate trying to score a run. *(See Fig 16 on page 28.)*

This list of equipment may seem daunting and rather discouraging for the beginner, or those only interested in a social game of

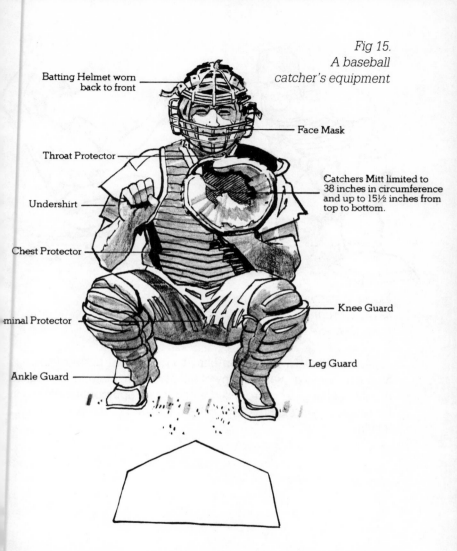

Fig 15.
A baseball
catcher's equipment

Batting Helmet worn
back to front

Face Mask

Throat Protector

Catchers Mitt limited to
38 inches in circumference
and up to 15½ inches from
top to bottom.

Undershirt

Chest Protector

Knee Guard

...minal Protector

Leg Guard

Ankle Guard

baseball in the park or on the beach. But if a more 'user-friendly' tennis ball is used, players need little if any protective equipment. However, this is not the case for those who intend progressing to play the game using a rubber baseball, of the type so popular in

27

*Fig 16. A catcher gathers the ball
as a base runner slides
towards home plate*

Japan, let alone a regulation hard ball. It would be most unwise for a catcher to go without any of his protective clothing, for others on the fielding team to play without an appropriate glove on his non-throwing hand, or for batters to stand at the plate without a helmet.

CHAPTER FOUR

PLAYING SKILLS

FITNESS AND PRACTICE

Amateur baseball is now played in more than 80 countries in all six continents, while professional baseball is played in Japan, South Korea and five countries in Latin America. However, few would argue that many of the best players in the world are those professionals who represent the 12 clubs of the National League, or the 14 clubs of the American League in the USA and Canada. Consequently, most of the examples in this book will feature players from these two major leagues.

Although the emphasis in baseball is on skills, players need specific training to perform to the best of their ability and reduce the risk of injury due to inadequate conditioning. Steve Carlton, the Philadelphia pitcher, is said to attribute his increased success since 1979 to positive thinking, karate, strength and flexibility training – and not talking to the media. Players do not succeed without regular purposeful practice, developing individual skills that will become second nature under pressure during a game. In the major leagues, players go for Spring training to Florida (Grapefruit League), California and Arizona (Cactus League). The Los Angeles Dodgers' training facilities at Vero Beach, Florida are considered to be the best in US professional sports.

Pitchers and catchers tend to need the most pre-season practice. No team can do well if these players are weak. Others would add that a team must be strong 'up the middle', i.e. the catcher, shortstop 2nd baseman and centrefielder. A team also needs 'power at the corners' i.e. 1st and 3rd basemen, who are picked not only for their batting ability but also for their fielding prowess. That only leaves two positions – right field and left field – but competition is so strong in the major leagues that these players tend to be as talented as the others.

In 1985 the average major leaguer's salary was nearly $400,000. So it is hardly surprising that the game attracts some of the best athletes in the world. Many were successful at other sports and could have made them their chosen profession. Kirk Gibson (Detroit) was an All-American wide receiver at Michigan State and drafted by the St Louis Cardinals of the NFL; Dave Winfield was drafted by clubs in the NFL, basketball's NBA and old ABA. Danny Ainge of the Boston Celtics played baseball in the major leagues for Toronto before turning to basketball.

THE PITCHER

It has been said that the game of baseball is at least 75 per cent pitching. For although every fielding position has its importance and every batter the opportunity to score runs, the influence of a good pitcher on a game is far greater than might initially be

Fig 17. A pitcher's basic action as seen from 1st base

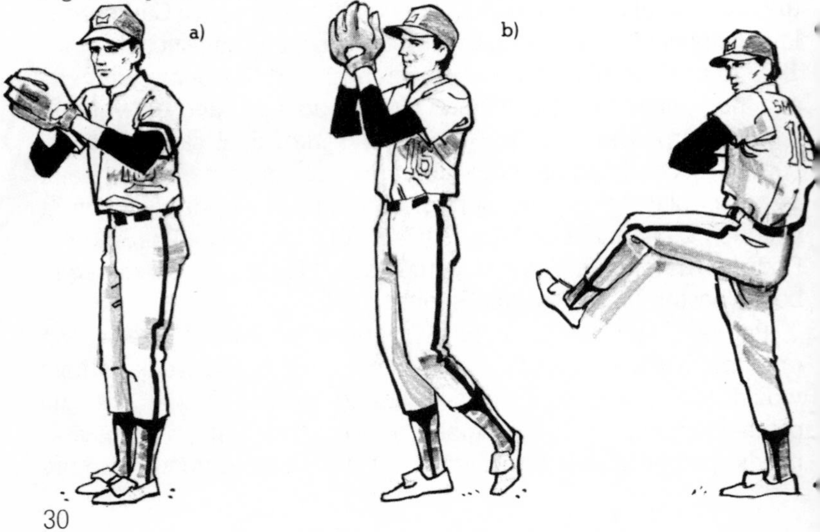

supposed. Consequently, pitchers tend to be treated as a special breed by coaches and fans alike. A pitcher should have strength in his legs, lower abdomen, back and shoulders. To pitch well he should develop his endurance, control, accuracy, and the ability to change his pace. He should also have the presence of mind to act quickly as an infielder in order to gather gentle taps that fall in front of the batter as a 'bunt', or catch top edges that loop towards the pitcher's mound.

The pitcher who is going to start the game will warm up about 15 minutes beforehand. Each pitcher develops his own routine of exercises then starts to throw, gently at first, then gradually increasing speed and purchase on the ball with his fingers to see which pitches are 'working' that day. This may be done in the 'bull pen', an area fenced off to the side of the field where pitchers practise in a world of their own. Starting pitchers, and relief pitchers (who are called into a game when the starter tires, loses control, or is replaced by a pinch hitter) practise throwing from a proper mound to a catcher behind a plate, in an attempt to imitate the game situation.

As with a bowler in cricket each pitcher has his own pitching

Fig 18. A pitcher's basic action as seen by the batter

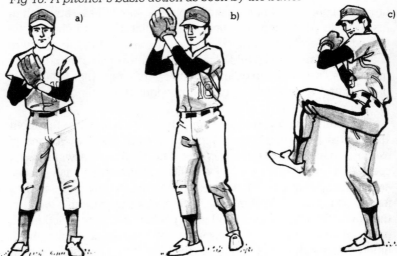

action. Some manage to adopt quite extraordinary positions as they strive to throw the ball into the batter's strike zone with a particular flight and at a certain speed. Although it is hard to generalise about this most individual of skills there are a few basic stages of the action which can be pinpointed. *(See Figs 17 and 18.)* Having decided, by means of signals given by the catcher, what pitch he is to throw, the pitcher grips the ball appropriately, hiding it from the batter in his fielding glove. He then stands in his starting position on the mound, sideways on to the batter, with his back foot (the pivot foot) touching the pitcher's rubber. He then starts his wind-up by shifting his weight onto his back foot and raises both arms above his head, still keeping the ball shielded from the batter.

There must then be a stop in the action, before he lifts his front leg to keep his balance while drawing back his throwing hand, and then starts to move his weight forward on to his front leg with a bent knee. The pitcher tries not to open his body and hips towards the batter too soon in this stride forward, as this reduces power and body action. The forward motion is helped by the fact that the pitcher is carried down the front slope of the mound.

Once the ball passes the pitcher's head and the front foot establishes a firm base, the throwing arm, wrist, and finally the fingers, snap the ball forward. Whatever the pitch, the upper arm should always be parallel with the ground as the ball is released, or power will be lost. The angle of the forearm will vary with the pitcher and each pitch. For straight overarm pitching the forearm is at 90 degrees to the ground, whereas for sidearm pitching it will be almost parallel with the ground. The pitcher should then follow through by swinging his rear leg forward, pivoting over the front leg with a swing of the hips. Apart from making sure the pitch is completed powerfully, the follow-through moves the pitcher into a potential fielding position at the front of the mound.

This full pitching action has to be reduced if a runner is on 1st base. The lengthy wind-up of arms and legs as the pitcher coils his body, as if tightening a spring, may give an alert runner time to steal a base. Therefore many pitchers will 'work out of the stretch', a position where both legs are planted and so making it easier to delay a runner. Most pitchers develop moves in their pitching action that make the runner think he is safe to run, or moves that lull him into thinking the pitcher is about to throw to his base. However, a pitcher should not allow these antics to distract him from getting the batter out. As a left-handed pitcher is facing 1st base when he stands on the mound, and does not have to turn his body to throw there, he is at an advantage over a right-hander.

Pitchers do not get it all their own way. Once he has started his pitching motion he cannot stop and throw to a base in order to catch a runner. If the pitcher does so, it is likely to be called a balk, which allows all base runners to advance one base. However, some umpires are more likely to call a balk in these circumstances than others. About 300 balks are called each major league season, but twice as many are ruled by National League umpires, perhaps because base runners are more aggressive in that league.

Each of the following sections outlines a basic pitch. However, just as no two bowlers hold the ball in the same way, each pitcher will evolve his grip for each pitch by trial and error.

A good pitcher tries to surprise and fool the batter by mixing his pitches but delivering them with as similar an action as possible. The pitch is selected by the catcher, although the pitcher may disagree and 'shake-off' the selection with a shake of his head. Once the pitch is decided the signal may be relayed to the fielders, so that they have some idea of what is meant to happen next.

The **Fastball** is, as the name suggests, a pitch thrown in order to overpower the batter by sheer pace. There are two main grips, both with the index and middle fingers on top and the thumb beneath. *(See Figs 19a and 19b.)*

a) With the seams. The fingers are each side of the writing on the ball. This pitch is meant to sink in flight, so it is more likely to be hit along the ground. Pitchers favour it in ball parks with grass infields, rather than those with artificial turf where the ball bounces higher.

b) Fingers across the seams, called a '4 seamer'. It appears to rise in flight but in fact the back spin on the ball helps make it slower to drop than other pitches.

Pressure from the index finger moves the ball in to a left-hander. Pressure from the middle finger moves the ball in to a right-handed batter. There is no fixed rule about gripping the ball: reliever Bruce

Change up (slower ball)
Fig 19a.

Fastball across the seams
Fig 19b.

Fig 20. The pitcher hides his grip on the ball with his glove

Fastball with the seams
Fig 21.

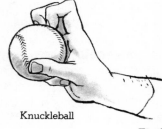

Knuckleball
Fig 22

35

Sutter (Atlanta) has a split finger grip, while Nolan Ryan (Houston) grips his fastball tightly and deep in the fingers, which is the traditional grip for a slower ball or change-up. *(See Fig 21.)*

The **Curveball** is a pitch which curves in the air. The aim is to outwit the batter with movement rather than speed. The ball is held between thumb and index finger, and pitched with a snap of the wrist so that it spins when it leaves the index finger. This tight spin induces the ball to break downwards and sideways. A right-handed pitcher makes it curve to the left, while a left-handed pitcher will make it curve to the right.

The **Slider** is a more recently named pitch, a cross between a fastball and a curveball. As the slider is thrown harder than the curveball it breaks less and later in flight, which makes it more difficult for the batter to detect. Left-hander Steve Carlton (Philadelphia) throws it well by not turning the wrist over completely, but by cutting the ball slightly as it leaves the finger tips, off-centre.

The **Knuckleball** tends to be the most difficult pitch to control, the hardest to hit and the most difficult for a catcher to gather cleanly. Phil Niekro (Yankees) has thrown the knuckleball for over 30 years but still does not know how it works! The ball is held between thumb and the knuckles of two or three fingers. It is thought not to spin in flight and therefore makes unpredictable turns or jumps as the seams catch the air flow. It works best in hot, humid conditions and when released rather than thrown. If pitched too hard it tends to 'flatten out' and becomes easy to hit.

Batters who have to face a proficient knuckleball pitcher not only have problems adjusting the timing of their swing to hit slower deliveries, but also tend to have problems readjusting to the faster speed of other pitchers in later innings, or during their next game.

The **Screwball** is effectively the curveball in reverse. A right-handed pitcher rolls the ball over the middle finger with a twist of the wrist so that the palm of his hand ends up pointing towards 3rd base. The spin given to the ball makes it swerve to the right. One of the few present-day major leaguers who has mastered this difficult pitch is Fernando Valenzuela (L.A. Dodgers).

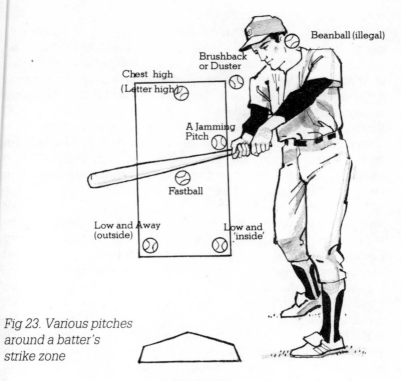

Fig 23. *Various pitches around a batter's strike zone*

Labels in figure:
Beanball (illegal)
Brushback or Duster
Chest high (Letter high)
A Jamming Pitch
Fastball
Low and Away (outside)
Low and 'inside'

Aiming the Pitch

Good pitchers try to throw the ball low in the strike zone aiming at the batter's weaker side (inside or outside). Low pitches tend to be more difficult to hit than higher deliveries. Even if hit, they are more likely to be grounders than line drives or fly balls. If a pitcher has not faced a particular batter before, he can look at how the batter stands in the batter's box for clues. If he stands away from the plate he may not like an inside pitch. Standing deep in the box may imply he will wait for any curveball to break. Standing at the front of the box suggests that he prefers to hit the ball before it breaks. If teams meet regularly during a season there should be some pre-game discussion of their opponents' strengths and weaknesses, and some realistic tactics should be decided. ('Smoke 'em low and outside' is not realistic.)

Few batters score a hit more than once in every three times at bat so the advantage is with the pitcher. A pitcher is also at an advantage over the batter if he can 'keep ahead of the count', that is, throw more strikes than balls. After three strikes the batter is out, but after four balls he is awarded 1st base. It is a dispiriting experience to 'walk' a batter in that way as it gives him a chance to score a run through the pitcher's lack of control, rather than through his skill with the bat. Sometimes, if a batter is in good form or the game situation dictates, the manager may instruct the pitcher to walk the batter on purpose, giving him 1st base on four balls, rather than risk an extra-base hit.

In the major leagues, starting pitchers usually pitch every four or five days. Relievers, who may only pitch a few innings, tend to pitch more often. The best relievers, such as Dan Quisenberry (Kansas City), might appear in every other game during the season. The increasing use of relief pitchers since the mid-1960s has improved the chance of major league pitchers having a longer career at the top. Even so, many great young pitchers in recent years, such as Don Gullett, Mark Fidrych and Rawly Eastwick, have faded from the game through injury. In the American League since 1972, the designated hitter rule has helped pitchers achieve more completed games than in the National League. The designated hitter bats instead of the starting and relieving pitchers. This gives the throwers a better opportunity to rest and concentrate on pitching, but also means that some pitchers, such as Jack Morris (Detroit) or Danny Jackson (Kansas City) have rarely batted in their major league careers.

Learning to Pitch

Any beginner contemplating becoming a specialist pitcher must think of the task as similar to that facing the specialist bowler in cricket. Both activities involve many hours of lonely, tiring practice in order to groove an effective grip and action. A pitcher with 'good stuff', who can move the ball in flight, and throw pitches consistently in the strike zone at whatever speed, usually sees his hard work rewarded as the opposition panic and swipe at thin air.

A young pitcher must not throw for too long at a time. Having warmed up properly he should try to throw the ball accurately, and with control, over the correct distance for his age group.

A good way for a young pitcher to learn, is to throw at the four corners of a strike zone chalked on a wall or garage door. Few have the natural ability to overpower batters with their pitching speed alone. Those who try, risk painful arm and shoulder injuries, particularly if tempted to throw curveballs at a young age. Once confident of his control, he should experiment with the grip and action on release of the ball, while varying the speed of his pitching, with as little change to his delivery action as possible.

A pitcher who throws knuckleballs is probably least likely to suffer overuse injuries. The knuckleball also has the potential to devastate a team's batting in the way a good leg-spinner may at cricket. However, like a poor leg-break, a poor knuckleball is an open invitation to any batter.

THE CATCHER

The qualities that make a good baseball catcher are the same as those for a good wicket-keeper, plus the ability to throw the ball powerfully and accurately. The catcher must be strong, steady, quick, agile, have good concentration, and be ever alert to moves and ploys during the game by his own side and the opposition. Unlike the wicket-keeper, the catcher is the only fielder who has a view of the whole field so should therefore be a leader, prepared to give positional advice to his fellow fielders. This may be done by means of signals from his position in the catcher's box behind home plate, or when the catcher asks the umpire to call 'Time' then walks to the mound to talk with the pitcher and infielders. The catcher should study batters closely, recognise any weaknesses or preferences during their turns at bat and pass these on to the pitcher and infielders. The catcher's signals will vary from team to team and with each pitcher's capabilities.

Fig 24 illustrates four signs and how the catcher's hand signals are shielded from the prying eyes of the next batter in the on-deck circle, and opposition coaches who stand near 1st and 3rd bases, by hiding his throwing hand with his large catcher's mitt and by putting one knee forward. Before the game, and again before each inning, pitcher and catcher should decide which of the signs given will be the real one, and which will be red-herrings. This deception is particularly important when a runner is on 2nd base as he will have a direct view of the catcher's signals to the pitcher.

The catcher should always call a pitcher's best pitches. When knuckleball pitcher Phil Neikro started with Atlanta, he suffered because the catchers were reluctant to call his best pitch. They could not catch the knuckleball cleanly and did not relish being dubbed 'retrievers' when the ball got away from them towards the screen 60 feet behind home plate. Neikro was sent down to the minors for a while until Bob Uecker, and later, Bruce Benedict were prepared to specialise in catching the unpredictable pitch as their way into the major leagues.

Once the pitch has been decided, the catcher gives another signal indicating where in the strike zone he wants the ball thrown. *(See Fig 25.)* The diagram of the batter's strike zone on page 37 has a number of typical pitches shown.

Strange as it may seem to those unfamiliar with baseball, the catcher needs all his protective clothing. Some pitchers not only pitch extremely fast, but the hard ball may be deflected by the bat or bounce in the dirt. Just before the pitcher pitches, the catcher should offer him a target of the strike zone to aim at with his knees, mitt and throwing hand. Then the depressed pocket of the mitt should face the pitcher, with the catcher's bare throwing hand out of the way to one side (but not behind his back), ready to gather the ball as it hits the mitt. He should not be tempted to leave his bare hand near the mitt or will risk suffering a severely bruised or broken finger. *(See Fig 26.)*

The catcher usually works from a crouching position behind home plate, to gather pitches and give the pitcher his signals. To avoid a balk being called by the umpire, the catcher must remain in the catcher's box until the ball leaves the pitcher's hand. His

Fig 24. Catcher's signals for four different pitches

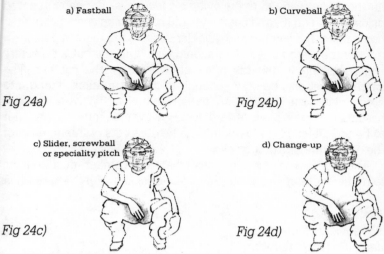

a) Fastball

Fig 24a)

b) Curveball

Fig 24b)

c) Slider, screwball
or speciality pitch

Fig 24c)

d) Change-up

Fig 24d)

*Fig 25. Catcher's signals suggesting where
in the strike zone the pitch should be aimed*

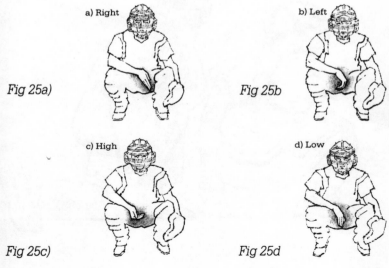

a) Right

Fig 25a)

b) Left

Fig 25b

c) High

Fig 25c)

d) Low

Fig 25d

weight should be forward but evenly distributed on both feet, and he should be ready to throw away his face mask (far enough not to risk stepping on it), and catch any foul balls which come down near home plate. If a catcher and infielder converge to catch a pop-up in front of the plate the infielder should take it, as the ball's trajectory will be taking it towards him but away from the catcher. The catcher must also be brave enough to tag out runners sliding into home plate, run forward to gather bunts, or back up the 1st baseman on most plays at 1st base. However, he must be wary not to be too quick off the mark in case he obstructs or interferes with the batter runner's progress.

There are particular situations where the catcher must be alert to runners attempting to steal a base. For example, if the batter has

Fig 26.
A rear view of the catcher
and home plate umpire

taken two balls and one strike a runner on 1st base may attempt to steal 2nd base. If the runner goes, then the catcher has to gather the pitch, rise and hurl the ball nearly 130 feet, over the pitcher's mound to 2nd base. A good base-runner can get from 1st to 2nd base in just over three seconds, while the fastest combination of pitcher and catcher will take a fraction of a second longer to throw the ball to 2nd base, so the advantage is with the runner. However, the best catchers, such as Gary Carter (Mets), can often succeed in catching the runner off base with this most skilful, spectacular play. As most batters are right-handed, left-handed catchers are at a disadvantage in attempting this move, as they have to move further to the right in order to avoid the batter before throwing to 2nd base. At present there are no left-handed catchers in the major leagues.

INFIELDERS

In recent years the level of athleticism in virtually all sports has been rising. This is especially true of baseball, with its enormous financial rewards. Nowadays it is not sufficient for a player to be able to bat but not field well, and the standard of fielding is constantly improving.

The catcher and pitcher are bracketed as a unit called the battery, while the 1st, 2nd and 3rd baseman and shortstop are bracketed as the infield. Infielders know that any type of ball may be hit at them, and are expected not only to gather it quickly but also throw it on to another infielder if there is a chance of putting out a base runner.

Infielders should crouch ready for the ball, keeping their hands off their knees but with their glove near the ground, as it is easier and quicker to rise for a hop or a catch than it is to go down for a low skidding grounder. Many infielders move slightly to their weaker side as they prepare to field. This makes it easier to move their feet around the ball while preparing to throw.

When fielding the ball an infielder should never point the fingers of his glove directly at the ball. When fielding grounders the glove fingers should point down, but when fielding or catching high balls

Fig 27. An infielder crouches ready to move in any direction

the glove's fingers should be pointing upwards. Once the ball has been watched right into the glove it should be gathered immediately with the bare throwing hand, while drawing both hands into the stomach and shifting the feet into an appropriate firm stance, ready to throw to one of the three bases or home plate in an attempt to put out any runners.

When fielding the ball backhanded on the non-glove side, the fielder almost turns his back on the batter. *(Fig 28.)* It is not wise to throw the ball backhanded, nor spin round to throw. It may look slick, but the player risks being disorientated and throwing the ball wide of the base. Sometimes in this disposition it is easier and quicker for a fielder to gather the ball barehanded before throwing it to a base. If in any doubt, a fielder should hold on to the ball, as every throw carries the possibility of an error.

Fig 28. An infielder gathers the ball backhanded, on his non-glove side

Each game has official scorers. In the major leagues these may be pressmen, with years of experience in the game. In days gone by they were more likely to spare fielders blushes after a poor piece of play and award a hit to the batter rather than an error against the fielder. Today they are far less generous, but an indication of how much fielding has improved in the majors is given by the fact that official errors have halved over the past 80 years.

The **1st baseman** crouches ready to field the ball as close to 1st base as convenient. This gives him a better chance to tag out the base runner, or, once he is at the base, to stop the runner stealing

Note the position of 1st Base on line

Fig 29. A right-handed 1st baseman is at a disadvantage if he has to relay the ball to another baseman

from 1st to 2nd base. He is allowed to wear a larger fielding mitt than the other infielders as he has to field so many hard throws. It is an advantage if the 1st baseman is tall, agile and left-handed, as for example, Keith Hernandez (Mets); in fact, over one in four of 1st basemen in the major leagues are left-handed. This is because as most throws go to his right-hand side when standing with one foot on 1st base, he can save time by not having to change the position of his feet before throwing to another fielder with his left hand.

Although the 1st baseman does not have to be as athletic as other infielders it is a mistake to attempt to 'hide' a weak fielder in this position.

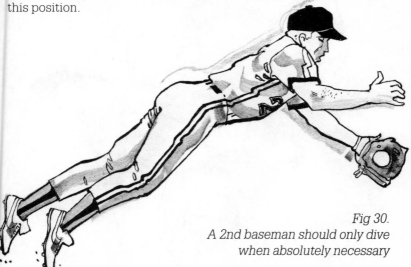

Fig 30.
A 2nd baseman should only dive
when absolutely necessary

The **2nd baseman** stands a few feet away from 2nd base on the 1st base side. The shortstop will help him cover 2nd base when he is called upon to field the ball, and he in turn must cover the 1st baseman when that fielder runs towards home plate to field a bunt.

The 2nd baseman should be expert at catching or gathering the ball quickly and then shifting his attention immediately to tagging out any base runners. He will often have to throw quickly across his body, having run in to field a grounder, so not surprisingly, there are no left-handed 2nd basemen in the majors. When attempting to

47

Fig 30a.
The 2nd baseman
throws to 1st base to
complete a double play

make a double play (where two of the opposition are dismissed on one play), the fielder will move over the base and touch it with his right foot, catch the throw (putting one man out), then throw the ball on, usually to 1st base, for the second out. *(Fig 30a.)* As the fielder throws he may have to jump high into the air to avoid the incoming runner sliding into 2nd base.

2nd base is a most important position. In the 1974 World Series Oakland's 2nd baseman Dick Green got no hits in 14 times at bat, yet saved three games for his team with his fielding, and narrowly missed being voted the Most Valuable Player on either side.

The **3rd baseman** does not handle the ball as often as the other infielders, does not run about as much as the 2nd baseman or shortstop, and does not tag out as many runners. However, it is not called the 'hot corner' for nothing. The 3rd baseman must be able to catch or gather the wide variety of balls hit hard in his direction near the left foul line. To widen their sphere of influence most 3rd basemen are on the move forwards or backwards (depending on the hitting situation) as the ball is pitched. As he has to throw the ball forwards or to his left it is an advantage if the 3rd baseman is right-handed. (There is only one left-handed baseman in the majors.) One of the finest fielders ever, in any position, was the 3rd baseman for the Baltimore Orioles between 1955-77, Brooks Robinson.

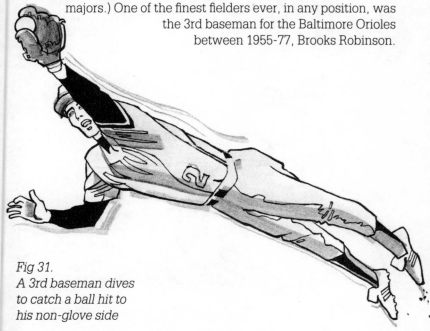

Fig 31.
A 3rd baseman dives
to catch a ball hit to
his non-glove side

The **Shortstop** is usually the best fielder in the team, a livewire specialist such as Ozzie Smith (St Louis), who may well be worth his place in the side for his fielding alone. He should be fast on his feet, able to catch and gather a wide variety of balls, and throw them quickly on to the appropriate fielder for each situation. The shortstop must be expert at tagging out base runners and needs a strong, accurate, reliable throw to complete double-plays. He should also help his outfielders by acting as a relay man, gathering their throw-ins and firing the ball quickly to the catcher or appropriate baseman. He may also relay pitching signals to the outfielders.

Fig 32. Despite the efforts of the incoming runner to stop him the shortstop prepares to complete a double-play at 1st base

Infielders' Practice Drills

A well-organised infield can make up for certain deficiencies in individual strength or athleticism through slick fielding and quick, accurate throwing. To help infielders become a cohesive unit and more likely to complete plays successfully under pressure, there are any number of permutations of infield fielding drills that can be practised before taking the field, briefly at the start of an inning, or between batters.

In the first, the ball is hit sharply along the ground usually with a light, fungo bat to the first player listed, who gathers the ball on his glove side and relays the ball on around the circuit:

a) 3rd base, 2nd base, 1st base, catcher, 3rd base, and back to the catcher.
b) shortstop, 2nd base, 1st base, catcher, shortstop, back to catcher.
c) 2nd base, shortstop, 1st base, catcher, 2nd base, back to catcher.
d) 1st base, shortstop, 1st base, to catcher.
e) catcher, shortstop, 1st base, to catcher.

This second rotation helps fielders practise double-play situations, once the first fielder listed has fielded the ball hit to his non-glove side:

a) 3rd base, 1st base, catcher, 3rd base, 2nd base, 1st base, and back to the catcher.
b) shortstop, 1st base, catcher, shortstop, 3rd base, to catcher again.
c) 2nd base, 1st base, catcher, 2nd base, 3rd base, and back to the catcher.
d) 1st base, shortstop, 1st base, to catcher.
e) catcher throws to 1st base, shortstop and back to the catcher.

Besides helping the confidence and cohesiveness of the fielding side, the significance of a well executed infield drill will not be lost on a batting side watching from their bench. By the same token, a sloppy infield drill does wonders for a base runner's confidence.

OUTFIELDERS

The three outfielders are equivalent to deep fielders in cricket. They should make allowance for the direction and strength of any breeze, the angle of the sun, the amount of bounce the ball takes from the grass or artificial turf, the position of the warning track near the outfield fence, and any obstructions or footholds in the wall or fence. As the pitch is delivered, the outfielders should move forward a few steps so that they are not caught flat-footed, keeping

Fig 33.
In only three steps the outfielder
has caught the ball and thrown it
in to a baseman, or the
cut-off man

in a semi-crouch so that they can break quickly towards the ball. To avoid the risk of collisions, injuries, and dropped catches fielders converging on a fly ball should call their name clearly. Never just 'Mine' or 'Yours' or the ball might drop harmlessly for extra bases and an error. An outfielder who has shown he is a quick runner and has a good arm is less likely to be pressurised by base runners, which gives him slightly more time to complete his tasks safely.

Many outfielders are better batters than fielders, but the outfield is no place to hide someone if the team is to be successful. Outfielders make fewer and less complicated plays than infielders, but against that they are expected to make fewer errors. Outfielders should only dive for catches if the game situation warrants it, otherwise their flashy efforts may prove costly for the team.

An outfielder should watch for the shortstop relaying the catcher's pitching signals and move accordingly at the last moment. Less gifted fielders can make up for their deficiencies by being alert to the various game situations as they arise. For example, if a runner is on base and the outfielder does not have time to throw out a runner with a relayed throw to home plate, he would do better to concede the run and throw to 2nd base instead, as at least that denies the hitter an extra base hit. Another situation to watch for is if scores are tied in the 9th inning, with two men out and one on base. As an extra base hit will score the winning run, the outfielders should play slightly deeper than usual. However, if the base runner is on 2nd base instead the outfielders should move in to catch the fly ball or throw a grounder direct to home plate to put out the potential winning run.

The **Leftfielder** must be a reliable catcher and brave enough to catch fly balls outside the left foul line, which may involve him risking leaning over into the stands. He must be a fast runner to field grounders, and have a strong arm to throw to 2nd or 3rd base, or to the relay man.

The leftfielder is busiest when right-handed power hitters are at bat, as they tend to pull the ball across their bodies into left field.

The **Centrefielder** is usually the best and most active outfielder, collecting line drives, fly balls and 'Texas Leaguers' (fly balls which drop between the infield and outfield). He must back up the 2nd baseman and shortstop and field any balls they miss. One of the best in the major leagues is Gary Pettis (California Angels) who is quick enough to cover much of his fellow outfielders' territory as well.

The centrefielder will shift around to the left or right depending on the hitter's suspected strengths, or move in if the player at bat is not a powerful hitter. The average batter is more likely to hit the ball between the infield and outfield than over an outfielder's head.

The **Rightfielder** must catch or gather fly balls in right field and outside the right foul line. He is busiest when left-handed power hitters are batting, as they tend to pull the ball across their bodies into right field. He must have a particularly strong arm as base runners often attempt to run after a catch is made in deep right field, realising it is a long throw from right field to 3rd base where it is vital to hold or put out a runner.

54

THE BATTER

The qualities that make a baseball player an effective batter are the same as those that bring success in any fast-moving ball game which requires hand-eye co-ordination, be it cricket, hockey, or squash.

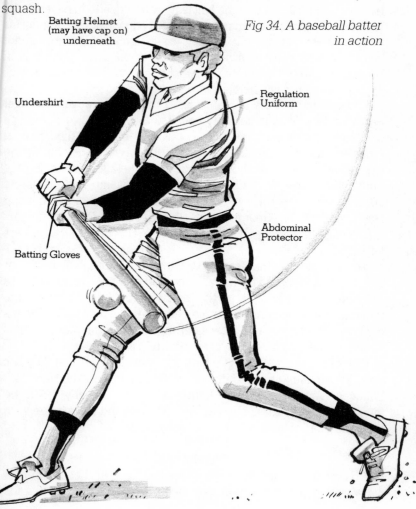

Batting Helmet
(may have cap on)
underneath

Undershirt

Batting Gloves

Regulation
Uniform

Abdominal
Protector

Fig 34. A baseball batter in action

The batter must stand in one of the rectangular batter's boxes, on either side of home plate, batting either right- or left-handed, i.e. holding the bat to the right or left side of the body. The white lines of the batter's box are considered part of the batter's territory, but if one or both of the batter's feet touch the ground outside the batter's box he is out and the ball is declared 'dead'. In baseball the width of the white lines marking the field are considered in play (as in rounders), and not out of play (as in cricket). Batters cannot switch from one batter's box to the other once the pitcher is in position to pitch. One in ten major leaguers is a switch hitter. This means he can bat effectively left- or right-handed.

Left-handed batters are considered to be at an advantage over right-handers. This is not only because they stand in the batter's box which is closer to 1st base, but also because their natural tendency is to pull the ball across their body when they hit, taking the ball away from the 3rd base side of the field and so forcing the outfielder to throw further for any deeply hit ball. It is no coincidence that a number of the best modern batters in the major leagues, such as George Brett (Kansas City), Don Mattingley (Yankees), Dave Parker (Cincinnati) and Wade Boggs (Boston) are left-handed.

To a cricketer, the frantic swinging of a baseball batter at waist-high full tosses seems an unskilled activity. However, once the sceptic is standing in the batter's box holding that slim, rounded bat it does not seem so easy. While every hitter has his own style, batting coaches consider there are certain fundamentals which will help a player improve his batting average.

One of the most successful batting coaches of the past 20 years was Charlie Lau, who died in 1984 while coaching at the New York Yankees. When he was at Kansas City in the early 1970s he influenced great hitters such as George Brett and Hal McRae with his basic rules of hitting, outlined briefly here.

The Stance

The batter should always stand relaxed, holding his head still, with his weight more on his back foot. Depending on where he intends

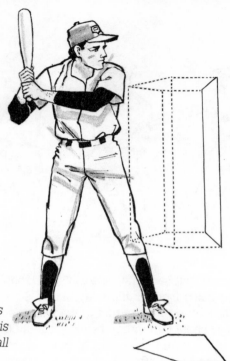

The batters
strike-zone
shown in
3 dimensions

Fig 35.
A batter stands
ready to start his
swing at the ball

hitting the ball, he adopts one of three basic batting positions. To make it easier to hit the ball up the middle of the field, he may stand with both feet parallel to home plate. Alternatively, to hit inside and outside pitches, the front foot may be moved closer to home plate than the back foot. Finally, to make it easier to pull the ball across his body or to stand square in order to bunt the ball, the front foot may be moved away from the plate opening the body towards the pitcher.

Hitting the Ball

Having decided on the stance that suits the situation, the player should hold the bat firmly, though not too tightly, as if preparing to swing an axe two-handed at a tree. Lau thought the bat's barrel should be gently touching the shoulder to help keep the hands back when swinging forward.

As the ball is pitched, the batter should keep his head still, watching the ball's flight until as late as possible, then shift his weight forward, lifting his front foot into a short step towards the ball. The batter should not bring his hips round too soon or he will lose power in the swing. The arms and hands should follow in a slightly downward arc with the arms fully extended while rolling the wrists on impact with the ball to snap the bat out in front of the plate. *(See Fig 36.)*

The batter should then follow through fully, by bringing the bat right round and releasing the lower hand from the handle. If all has gone to plan, the batter should then drop the bat from his top hand before heading for 1st base with another hit to his credit.

The beginner should not be tempted to swing the bat up at the ball, nor heave too hard, throwing his head back with the effort. An old adage runs: 'Swing the bat down and your average goes up. Swing the bat up and your average goes down.'

Charlie Lau considered many modern players, particularly the young, were mistaken in following the vogue for heavy bats. He thought the extra weight made them stand with their hands held too high. Lau also considered many players took too long a step towards the pitch. He studied films of many great hitters and found

Fig 36.
Five stages of a
batter's swing
through the ball,
from his initial
stance to his
follow through

d)   e)

that although they each had idiosyncracies in their swings, they had one thing in common. They kept the step and the swing of the arms separate. The two movements did not overlap.

The trajectory the ball takes when hit is largely governed by the spin on the ball, the arc in which the bat is swung, and which part of the ball is hit. When the ball is hit above its centre line it travels down, bouncing along the ground (known as a 'grounder'). When hit along its centre line the ball travels straight and fast, and is called a 'line drive'. If hit below its centre line the ball flies up in the air and is known variously as a 'pop up', 'blooper', or 'fly ball'.

The direction in which the ball is hit is largely governed by timing, as that determines the angle of the bat barrel on impact with the ball. When a right-handed batter hits the ball too early, the angle of the bat often drags the ball towards (or outside) the left foul line. When he hits it too late, the angle of the bat pushes the ball towards (or outside) the right foul line.

Most beginners find it difficult to hit the ball away from the body as the natural tendency is to pull the ball across the body to the near side of the field. Pitchers anticipate this by trying to throw pitches that break away from the batter. Therefore, a batter who can consistently hit the ball away from him, to the 'opposite field', can be most successful at any level of baseball.

Those without access to a pitching machine, and players just starting to play the game, may gain useful practice using a hitting tee, which enables a player to feel what each hit is like. The tee can be adjusted to various heights to represent various pitches in the strike zone, and the player then hits the ball to particular areas of the field. If fielders are not available the ball may be tied to a length of string or hit into a net.

The Designated Hitter

During the past 15 years or so, the designated hitter rule has been adopted by an increasing number of organisations. The designated hitter bats instead of the starting pitcher and all relieving pitchers, but does not go out to field. Designated hitters may in turn be substituted by pinch hitters during the game. This specialisation, and the lack of fielding activity, has allowed players such as Hal McRae (Kansas City) to play several more seasons in the major leagues. It has also led to the more bulky designated hitters being unkindly referred to as designated eaters. The designated hitter rule is never used in the National League, and only used in the World Series in the American League team's ball park.

Bunting

All batters learn how to bunt, but few do it well. In order to bunt the batter takes his normal stance, but as the ball is pitched he slips the lower hand halfway down the bat barrel. Holding the bat loosely in front, nearly parallel to the ground (keeping his fingers behind the barrel of the bat), he allows the ball to hit the dead bat which absorbs most of the power so that the ball is bunted, rolling gently for about 20 feet just inside the 1st or 3rd base foul lines.

The aim is to catch the fielders back on their heels so that by the time the catcher, pitcher, 1st and 3rd basemen have decided who will field the ball, the batter is already running at top speed for 1st base. Intelligent bunting by a player such as Kirk Gibson (Detroit) can be extremely effective, even when the game situation makes it a fairly predictable option.

Fig 37. A left-handed batter has bunted the ball and is already setting off towards 1st base

Base running

Once the ball has been hit safely, the batter drops his bat and becomes a base runner. A base runner must touch each of the bases with one foot. Games have been lost merely because a runner forgot to touch a base.

The base runner should run directly between bases, but may take a curved run cutting across the inside edge of the base if he is going for an extra base, rather than trying to turn at 90 degrees. When running to 1st base a batter may over run the base after touching it and not be tagged out, but loses this immunity if the umpire considers he will attempt to go on to 2nd base. A fielder may then try to tag the runner out by touching him with the ball while the runner is still off base *(See Fig 38.)* At 2nd and 3rd base a runner must be more careful, if a fielder has the ball, as he is only safe with one foot in contact with the base. In two weeks during July 1985 Marty Barrett (Boston) tricked both Bobby Grich (Angels) and Doug DeCinces (Angels) into leaving their bases.

Fig 38. A base runner attempts
to avoid being tagged out
by a fielder

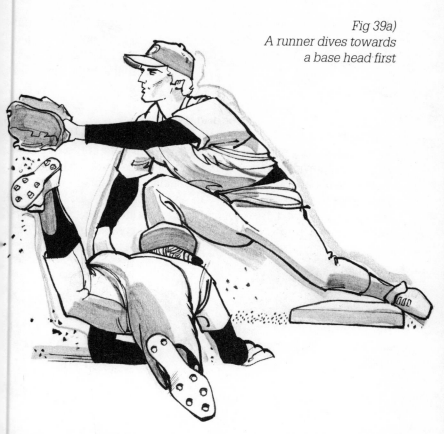

Fig 39a)
A runner dives towards
a base head first

There are two main ways in which a runner may arrive at a base when sliding into it. *(See Figs 39a and 39b.)*

a) sliding head first to touch the bag with a hand. This method is potentially dangerous, as the runner risks injury to head or hands, a painful stomach, and a face full of sand.

b) by throwing his feet out forwards, falling on hip and backside, and sliding in so that one foot will hit the bag.

If under pressure as he runs for home plate, the runner goes in feet first, aiming for the catcher's shinguards. When going for any base, the runner can knock the fielder off balance. This is a particularly useful tactic when one runner is caught in a potential double play as it may prevent one runner being put out. As a base runner must return to re-touch the base he has left after a fly ball has been caught, before he can advance to the next base, he should watch the 3rd base umpire signal the batter 'out' or 'safe'.

Stealing bases

A base runner does not have to wait until a batter hits the ball before trying to get to the next base. He may attempt to steal his way there, providing the ball has not been declared 'dead'. The runner 'takes a lead' by crouching, facing the pitcher, some 3½ steps from the base, so that he can dive back if necessary. His aim is to get to the next base safely before the pitcher or catcher can throw the ball to the relevant baseman. A base stealer from 1st base watches a right-handed pitcher's foot in case it moves

Fig 39b)
A runner slides into a base feet first
and rises ready to move on
if possible

a)   b)

towards 1st base. A left-handed pitcher's shoulder will give the first clue of a potential pick-off move.

Pitcher Phil Neikro (Yankees) is renowned for being able to lull runners at 1st base into a state of false security before hurling the ball to the 1st baseman to 'pick off' the runner. Beginners should not stray more than a step or two away from 1st base, and keep their eyes on the ball at all times.

Rickey Henderson (Yankees) stole a major league record 130 bases in 1982, but was caught stealing 24 per cent of the time. It has been reckoned that two successful steals are needed to make up for each time a base runner is caught stealing in the major leages, while four times out of five a hit would have brought the run home anyway. However, in the junior game and in the park, it is a far more productive skill, as the standard of fielding is not as high.

The Batting Line-up

Before a major league game each manager will hand copies of his batting line-up to the home plate umpire and to the opposing manager. The line-up is in strict batting order from 1 to 9 and may not be adjusted. However, substitutes may take the place of starting players in the line-up, though once a player has been replaced by a substitute he cannot return to play in that game.

The following lists a few qualities a manager looks for in individual batters:

No. 1 is the lead-off batter who does not have to be able to hit home runs. His main task is to get on base in whatever way he can, and so present a distraction for the fielding side. He may steal a base if the pitcher becomes too preoccupied with the batter at the plate, or provide a run-scoring threat from any deep-hit ball.

No. 2 should be good at hitting behind the runner on 1st base, and not hit into a double play. A quicker runner should bat ahead of a slower man, as if the faster runner is at first he will have a better chance of breaking up any double play. He may also be a good bunter.

No. 3 is often the best batter in the team, getting more turns at bat than No. 4. As another power hitter will be at 4, the pitcher cannot afford to pitch around him too often.

No. 4 is the 'clean-up hitter', a long ball hitter (or 'slugger') who can clear the bases by bringing home the base runners already aboard.

No. 5 is a less powerful batter, able to act as a clean-up hitter.

No. 6 needs qualities similar to the lead-off batter, because if the earlier clean-up hitters have been successful, the bases will be empty once more.

No. 7, 8 and 9 tend to be those players who are not specialist batters but worth their place in the team for other skills (e.g. the shortstop, catcher or pitcher). It is particularly useful if the 8th batter in the order can get on base. This means that the 9th batter has to bat in the same inning, which avoids the 9th (and usually weakest) batter becoming the lead-off batter (and, viewed realistically, the first out) in the next inning, when the top of the order is at bat.

If the 8th batter succeeds in getting on base, a common ploy is for the 9th batter to attempt to bunt the 8th man on to 2nd base, where he will represent a runscoring threat.

GAME SITUATIONS

There are a host of game situations that batting and fielding sides have to be prepared for. In the major leagues, the planning and execution only possible with skilled players, may be too sophisticated for younger players. However, here are a few of the more easily recognised plays.

Sacrifice Hit

As the name implies, this move involves the batter hitting the ball so that it will be caught by a fielder, but too far to stop one or more team mates on base advancing closer to home plate. To perform this play a batter must have the confidence and ability to undercut the ball on impact.

Sacrifice bunt

If there is a runner on 3rd base with only one out, the fielding side will move in to protect home plate, as this is an ideal situation for the batter to bunt the runner home to score. If the base runner sets off from 3rd base before the bunt is attempted it is called a sacrifice squeeze, because if the batter fails to connect with the ball the base runner is almost certain to be out.

This is a thrilling play, but as the standard of fielding in the major leagues is so high it only works about 40 per cent of the time. However, it proves a much more successful move in junior or recreational baseball where fielding errors are far more common.

Extra Base Hit

With a runner on 1st base, the aim is to advance that runner, when the hit is made, past 2nd base and on to 3rd base. The batter hits the ball towards an outfielder who throws to the shortstop (or 2nd baseman) who relays the ball on to 3rd base or home plate, depending on the speed of the runner from 1st base. Meanwhile, the batter should have reached 2nd base.

This play is profitable when the base runner is particularly fast, but otherwise it courts disaster.

Fig 40. Extra Base Hit

Force Play

A force play occurs where a base runner loses the right to occupy a base because the batter has become a base runner.

With a runner on 1st base, the batter hits a grounder so that the runner is forced to go on to 2nd base. The 2nd baseman gathers, or is thrown the ball, and puts a foot on 2nd base before the runner and so puts him out. He does not need to tag the runner in a force play. If he fields the ball too far off 2nd base, he may throw to the shortstop who will be covering 2nd instead.

Fig 41. Force Play

Double Play

This follows on from a force play. If the 2nd baseman or shortstop has put out a runner at 2nd base, and then throws quickly over or around the incoming runner to 1st base before the batter reaches 1st base, then that player is out as well. This is called a double play.

If the shortstop fields the ball and throws it on to the 2nd baseman, the double play is more difficult, as the 2nd baseman must gather the ball, tag the base, avoid the incoming runner, and throw the ball on to 1st base.

A double play is possible at any two bases, or a base and home plate; it requires a good nerve and great presence of mind from the 2nd baseman and shortstop.

Fig 42. Double Play

Hit and Run play

A base runner on 1st base is instructed to run for 2nd as soon as the ball is pitched. This will look like an attempt to steal from 1st to 2nd base, so the shortstop or 2nd baseman moves to cover 2nd base. This leaves one of them out of position; the batter then tries to hit the ball, whatever the pitch, into the gap left by the fielder.

If it works, the batter reaches 1st base and the base runner from 1st may get to 3rd base. A possible double play has been avoided and there are runners on 1st and 3rd base.

This play is especially productive against a tentative, poorly organised infield.

Fig 43. Hit and Run Play

Delayed Double Steal

The aim is for the fielders to outwit the two base runners (who consider the initiative is with them) as they attempt to steal two bases.

As the ball is pitched, the base runners on 1st and 3rd base set off to steal 2nd and home plate respectively. The catcher throws to 2nd base to pick-off one runner. This throw may be either: intercepted by the 2nd baseman who throws back to the catcher at home plate, to put out the incoming runner from 3rd base, or, is taken by the shortstop who puts out the runner at 2nd base. The clear priority is to put out the base runner going from 3rd base to home, otherwise he will score a run.

As this play requires a great deal of skill and practice it is not recommended for beginners.

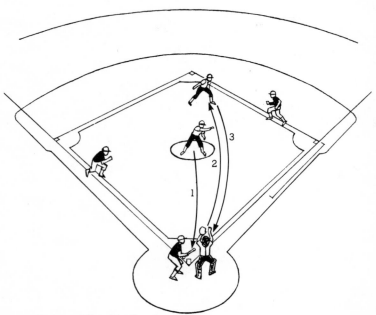

Fig 44. Delayed Double Steal

Squeeze play

This occurs only with a runner on 3rd base. The batter lays down a bunt which rolls about 25 feet down the 3rd base line, and the base runner on 3rd runs for home plate. This puts pressure on 3rd baseman and catcher, while the pitcher also runs towards the bunted ball.

What do the three fielders do? The 3rd baseman may be needed back at 3rd base in case the runner heads back to 3rd. The catcher will be needed to put out the runner at home plate. If the pitcher fields it, he must decide whether to throw to home plate, 3rd base, or 1st base. If there is any hesitation or delay, both runners will be safe, while if a fielder has to throw to 1st base the runner from 3rd base will score.

Triple Play

A triple play only occurs once or twice in a major league season, but is worth mentioning as it is so spectacular. It occurs when three players are out on a single play.

Very occasionally the triple play has been completed by one person, or unassisted. Ron Hansen did it for the Washington Senators against Cleveland in 1968, but the most famous instance was in game 5 of the 1920 World Series by Bill Wambsganss, 2nd baseman for Cleveland against the Brooklyn Dodgers. In the 5th inning, there were runners on 1st and 2nd base. Mitchell, the batter, hit a line drive which Bill caught (one out); the runners had kept running, mistakenly thinking the ball would go through for a hit. They then had to return, but Bill stepped on 2nd base (two out) to get Kilduff the player who was trying to double back from 3rd base. He then tagged out Miller, the runner from 1st base who was still heading for 2nd (three out).

THE UMPIRES

Umpires are responsible for the conduct of the game and for maintaining discipline on the field. Each umpire may also rule on any point not covered by the official rules of baseball. In the major leagues the umpires have wide powers, and may send off or eject any player, club official, or substitute from the playing field. Umpires may also have other people removed (e.g. spectators and media people), if they are considered to be preventing the umpires carrying out their duties.

Players cannot argue about 'balls' and 'strikes' but may appeal to the umpire in five situations when fielding:

a) where a team bats out of order
b) where a base runner fails to touch a base
c) where a base runner fails to return to 1st base immediately after over-running or over-sliding 1st base
d) where a batter misses a base when advancing or returning
e) where a base runner fails to tag up after a fly ball has been caught.

With so many split-second calls to be made during a game in so many areas of the field, it is too much to expect one umpire to control a game properly. An amateur game should have one umpire behind home plate to call balls and strikes as well as plays around home plate. A second umpire should stand out on the field, usually in the infield behind the pitcher's mound to the 1st base side, so that he is well placed to call any balk, plays at 1st base, and other plays in the infield or outfield.

In the major leagues umpires work in teams of four, and rotate their duties each game from home plate to 3rd base, to 2nd base to 1st base. Unlike in most sports, baseball umpires have no official signals for particular plays for the benefit of their colleagues, the players, scorers, or spectators. Each umpire team is asked to work out their own clear, simple set of signals for use in the game. However certain conventional signals have been adopted over the years, of which the most common are:

a) Play Ball: beckon to pitcher with bent right forearm.
b) Time Out: palm of hand straight out in front of body to stop the pitcher.
c) Out: point with a firm thrust of the hand to one side.
d) Safe: both arms straight out to the side with palms facing the ground.

e) Infield fly rule: right fist raised above head.

f) Dead Ball: both hands held straight above head.

The number of balls and strikes received by a batter should be shown by the home plate umpire holding up the appropriate number of fingers on each hand.

The **home plate umpire** calls balls and strikes, keeping a record of them and the number of outs in the inning on a hand held indicator. He keeps home plate clean, makes a note of all scoring, team changes, and replaces damaged baseballs from a black bag on his hip.

In the American League the home plate umpire stands behind the catcher's head; in the National League he stands behind the catcher but looks at the strike zone between the catcher and the batter.

Each umpire has his own definition of the strike zone and it does not take long for a player to discover what that is. In the major leagues the strike zone in the N.L. has tended to be some two inches lower than that of the A.L. This convention has had influences on the pitching in both leagues: N.L. pitchers realise they are more likely to have a low pitch around the knees called a strike than in the A.L., where a high pitch around the arm pits is more likely to be called a strike. This in turn has had an impact on batting in the two leagues. For example, in the N.L. (where seven of the twelve ball parks have had artificial turf) batters tend to swing at lower pitches, attempting to chop them into the ground and through or over the infield for a hit. This means that N. L. base runners are often more aggressive on the base paths as they attempt to break up any potential double play. A.L. hitters, on the other hand, tend to swing at higher pitches and hit more home runs.

The home plate umpire wears a heavy protective face mask with a throat protector, chest protector (worn inside or outside the blue, grey and black uniform), shinpads under his trousers and protection for his feet. (See drawing on page 42.)

The **3rd base umpire** stands about eight feet behind the base to judge close plays at 3rd, and half-swings by a left-handed batter. He has a sealed bag of over 40 baseballs to pass on to the plate umpire, all of which may be needed during a game, as once a ball is hit into the crowd it cannot be used again.

The **2nd base umpire** stands behind the base path between 2nd and 3rd, to judge close plays.

The **1st base umpire** stands behind and close to 1st base to judge close plays and any half-swing by a right-handed batter. In the World Series two extra umpires are employed, one each along the left and right foul lines. *(See Fig 8, page 16.)*

There are several plays that the umpires have to watch particularly closely, such as half-swings by the batter, close plays at the bases, the infield fly rule, double plays, tag plays, and whether the ball has been caught properly. Umpires must watch out for players attempting to cheat, especially in the following ways:

a) batters who prepare their bats illegally.

b) base runners who do not stay within the regulation distance of the base paths, or who slow down to block a fielder's view of the ball or another runner.

c) fielders who grab or obstruct a base runner, jump about to distract a batter, or prevent a batter from hitting a pitch.

d) catchers who touch a batter's bat as he swings, or fake tag-outs at home plate, or obstruct the runner when they are supposed to be catching a pop-up.

e) pitchers who balk on delivery, pitch before the batter is ready, who scuff or cut the ball's surface, or who throw spit balls tainted with a variety of substances hidden on their bodies, clothing or shoes. Indeed, pitchers tend to use almost anything but spit.

f) coaches who move outside the marked coaches' boxes to see the catcher's pitching signals.

THE MANAGER AND COACHES

The playing squad of a major league team is backed by a manager and up to half a dozen coaches who each concentrate on particular aspects of the game. The manager and coaches wear the team's uniform during the game.

The Manager

The manager has overall responsibility for the running of the team and takes most of the decisions on the field of play from his position on the bench. The home team manager may postpone a game due to bad weather but once the line-up has been handed to the umpire-in-chief, the umpire becomes the sole authority on starting and finishing play. A manager decides who plays, who will be the starting pitcher and any short or long relief pitchers that may be needed during the game, and is responsible for any positional changes, substitutes, pinch hitters or runners. Few active players have the experience or presence to be a successful manager. One of the rare exceptions currently playing in the major leagues is Pete Rose, manager of the Cincinnati Reds, a legend in his own lifetime, who holds the record for the most hits in a major league career.

The Coaches

Besides the manager, major league teams will have the luxury of at least four paid coaches with various responsibilities within the club on and off the field. During the game, one of them will be stationed in the 1st base coaching box and another in the 3rd base coaching box while their team is batting. From these positions they relay the manager's signals from the dugout and help base runners in particular ways. However, they may not interfere with play, nor distract the pitcher.

The **1st base coach** reminds the runner at 1st base of his options. He will point out the pitcher's pick-off moves and warn the runner where the 1st baseman is positioned.

The **3rd base coach** helps runners trying to move from 1st to 3rd base, or from 2nd to home plate. As the runner will probably be uncertain where the ball is, the coach indicates whether the runner should slide into 3rd (if it is going to be a close play), or can arrive standing up, or should keep running to home plate and attempt to score a run.

In Britain the manager will usually stand in the 3rd base coaching box while his team is at bat. The club's coach or perhaps a senior player will stand in the 1st base coaching box.

CHAPTER FIVE

MAJOR LEAGUE BASEBALL

The terms 'Major League Baseball' and 'Organised Baseball' include the activities of the twelve-club National League and the fourteen-club American League. Each February or March these 26 major league teams assemble squads of between 40 and 100 players for Spring training in the warmer climate of Florida, Arizona or California. During the following five or six weeks those players who have not been playing Winter baseball down in Latin America regain their fitness and playing skills, while young hopefuls and new signings are tried out in pre-season exhibition games against other major league clubs training in the area.

Before the regular season starts on 'Opening Day' in early April the squad must be cut down to 24 players. The remainder are released or sent down to one of the club's minor league farm system teams. Those sent down to the minors, play in leagues graded in ability from AAA, to AA, to A, to rookie leagues. Each major league club has between four and seven farm teams. Minor leaguers all hope that their good form, or perhaps injury to one of the 720 or so major league players, will give them an opportunity to prove themselves in the big leagues which attract over 46 million spectators each season.

Although American League and National League players may be traded from one league to the other, teams from the two leagues never meet in regular season competition. From early April until October the two leagues conduct their fixtures in total isolation. The only time a N.L. club may play a A.L. club is in pre-season exhibition games, Spring training, the Hall of Fame Game in July, or the World Series. Players from the two rival leagues will meet at the All-Star game each July if selected.

National League
(The 'Senior Circuit', organised 1876)

West Division

Atlanta Braves
Cincinnati Reds
Houston Astros
Los Angeles Dodgers
San Diego Padres
San Francisco Giants

East Division

Chicago Cubs
Montreal Expos
New York Mets
Philadelphia Phillies
Pittsburgh Pirates
St Louis Cardinals

Each of the twelve N.L. clubs listed above, plays the other five teams in the same division eighteen times during the season (nine times at home, nine times away). Each club also plays each of the six clubs in the other division twelve times during the season (six times at home and six times away). This regular season of 162 games takes place between early April and early October. When the regular season ends, the winners of the two divisions play off in a best of seven games series to decide the N.L. champions and the league's representatives in the World Series in mid-October.

American League
(The 'Junior Circuit', organised 1900)

West Division

California Angels
Chicago White Sox
Kansas City Royals
Minnesota Twins
Oakland A's
Seattle Mariners
Texas Rangers

East Division

Baltimore Orioles
Boston Red Sox
Cleveland Indians
Detroit Tigers
Milwaukee Brewers
New York Yankees
Toronto Blue Jays

● = National League
■ = American League

0   miles   6[

Fig 45. Map to show the 26 Major League clubs

The fourteen American League clubs listed above play a slightly more complicated regular season than the N.L. clubs. Each team plays three of the clubs in the same division fourteen times during the season (seven times at home and seven times away) but only plays the other three clubs in the same division twelve times (six times at home and six times away). They also play each of the seven clubs in the other division twelve times (six games at home and six games away). The post-season arrangements are the same as in the National League. The winners of the two divisions play-off in a best-of-seven-game series for the league championship and the honour of representing the A.L. in the World Series.

In both leagues Spring training and the regular season last some 33 weeks, and over half this time is spent away from home. If a player appears in all his club's games, but is not selected for the All-Star game he can expect only 19 days off during the season, and much of that time will be spent travelling to the next venue. The season lasts another three weeks for teams that qualify for post-season play-offs and the World Series. A number of players then play in the Winter leagues of Florida and Arizona from September until November, or play Winter baseball in Latin America from October to January. This is followed by a month or two's rest before they report for Spring training with their major league clubs.

Following Major League Baseball in Britain

The best way to gain up-to-date information about major league baseball from Britain is via the Armed Forces Radio and Television Service relayed by the American Forces Network Europe. Depending on local reception conditions, AFN Europe may be picked up on at least three Medium Wave frequencies (872, 1106, and 1142 kHz). Games rarely start before 1.00 pm on the East coast of the USA, which is after 6.00 pm British time. This is no bad thing as reception tends to improve as the night goes on. Night games, relayed from the West coast of the USA, will start after 2.00 am British time, and tend to have the best reception of all.

The highlight of the major league baseball season is the World Series, played from mid-October over the best of seven games. Each game may be watched on TV by over 65 million people in the USA, while millions more will be watching and listening around the world. In Britain recorded highlights have been screened for many years by ITV. With the advent of a fourth national TV network and various cable franchises (not to mention the prospect of satellite television) there will inevitably be more baseball screened in the UK over the next few years; this will in turn promote further the development of the domestic game. Channel Four Television screened 80 minutes of edited highlights of the 1985 World Series on New Year's Day 1986.

A couple of national daily newspapers in the UK (notably *The Daily Telegraph*, and *The Times*) already give baseball scores for the two major leagues, and from time to time may show the standings for the East and West divisions of the National League and American League. Beside each team is listed:

W = total wins so far in the regular season of 162 games.

L = total defeats suffered so far.

Pct = the percentage of games played that each team has won, calculated by dividing the total wins by the total games played.

GB = the number of games that each club is behind the divisional leader(s). This is the figure that most fans look for first, and shows the number of games that a team must win to achieve a percentage that is better than the current leader. Teams try to play well above .500 and not fall more than 10 games behind, although clubs that trail the leaders draw comfort from the exploits of the New York Giants in 1951. The Giants had been 13½ games behind the Brooklyn Dodgers with only six weeks of the National League's regular season remaining. They recovered to win 37 of their last 44 games and tied for first place with the Dodgers. The Giants then won the third and deciding play-off game between the clubs in the last half of the 9th inning. This sensational pennant race was the central theme for an episode of M.A.S.H., the bitter-sweet television series set in the Korean War.

SCORING A BASEBALL GAME

Major league baseball games have official paid scorers, appointed by the leagues. For over 100 years these scorecards have been summarised by newspapers as 'box scores'. It is relatively easy to score a game at the ball park or listening at home. Every amateur scorer develops a system of scoring that suits him, but a simple shorthand to record likely events during a game might include:

—	single	W/BB	walk/base on balls
=	double	IBB	intentional base on
≡	triple		balls
HR	home run	HP	hit by pitch
B	bunt	BK	balk
SAC	sacrifice/hit/fly/bunt	WP	Wild pitch

↖ ↑ ↗	(may be crossed with an arrow to show direction of hit)	PB	passed ball
		~	new pitcher
		K	strike out (swinging)
		Ʞ	strike out (called 3rd strike)
SB	stolen base	FC	fielder's choice
FO	forced out	F	fly ball caught
CS	caught stealing	PF	pop fly caught
E	error	FF	foul fly ball caught

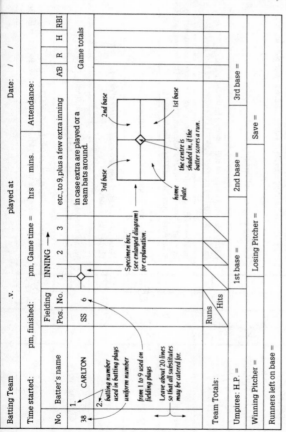

Fig 47. An example of a scorecard which could be constructed at home

83

Fig 48. A worked example of two innings batted by a team

#	Batter	INNING 1	INNING 2	EXPLANATION
1	CARLTON	(triple) ◆ 2	◇	Carlton hit a triple to left field.
2	ESSENDON	4 ↗	◇	Essendon singled to right, scoring Carlton (1 run). (So Essendon's batting number 2 goes in Carlton's home plate square)
3	COLLINGWOOD	① W	◇	Collingwood struck out swinging (1st out)
4	FITZROY	6-4 ② W	◇	Fitzroy was given a base on balls, moving Essendon to 2nd. (So Fitzroy's batting number 4 goes in Essendon's 2nd base square)
5	HAWTHORN	(6-4-3) ③	◇	Hawthorn hit a grounder to the short stop, who threw to 2nd baseman to force out Fitzroy (2nd out) 2nd baseman relayed to 1st baseman to get Hawthorn in the double play (3rd out) to end the 1st inning.
6	FOOTSCRAY	✕	P.F-2 ①	Footscray's pop-fly was caught by the catcher (1st out)
7	NORTH		CS ② E-6	North hit to the short stop who made an error allowing North to get on base.
8	RICHMOND	◇	(2-base)	With Richmond at the plate, North is caught stealing (2nd out) Richmond then hit a double to left field.
9	SWAN	◇	3-3 ③	Swan grounds to 1st baseman who tags Swan (3rd out) to end 2nd inning. Richmond is left on base. Carlton will bat first in the 3rd.

While these symbols vary, there is a standard set of fielders' numbers which are written on the scorecard to the right of the batter's name and used when giving details of fielding plays:

Battery		*Infielders*		*Outfielders*	
pitcher	1	1st baseman	3	leftfielder	7
catcher	2	2nd baseman	4	centrefielder	8
		3rd baseman	5	rightfielder	9
		shortstop	6	designated hitter	DH

In the A.L. the designated hitter is written into the batting order but the pitcher is not. For batting plays the player's number in the batting order is used.

One of the most common commercially produced scorecards has a divided box within the framework to represent a batter's progress around the bases. It shows what each batter does, and which fielders are involved in the plays. Each team has its own scorecard page and details are recorded as shown on the example.

If a batter reaches 1st base, the fact is recorded in the bottom right-hand corner of the box with a symbol showing how he got there. His progress around the bases is also noted.

When a batter is put out, the positional number (1 to 9) of the fielder that makes the put out, plus any assisting player(s) is/are written in a circle in the box, separated by a hyphen, with the appropriate abbreviation. The number of outs in the inning (up to three) is also put in a small circle in the appropriate player's box.

On a double play the details are listed in the box of the second batter put out and circled. The first batter in the double play is noted in the usual way.

For an unassisted put out, the positional number of the fielder handling the ball is written twice separated by a hyphen (e.g. 3-3).

In a put out by a rundown all the players who handle the ball are listed in the order they touch it, so the box can get rather crowded! When a player advances, thanks to the batter following him in the order, that player's batting number in the line up is placed in the appropriate quarter of the box.

CHAPTER SIX

BASEBALL AROUND THE WORLD

About sixty countries, with more than 100 million players, are affiliated to the International Baseball Association, which is the world ruling body of amateur baseball, recognised by the International Olympic Committee. Baseball will be a demonstration sport at the 1988 Olympic Games in Seoul, South Korea, the eighth occasion the game has been selected for this honour, and there is every chance that it will become a full medal sport from 1992. National leaders as politically diverse as President Ronald Reagan and Cuba's Premier, Fidel Castro, are for once united in their belief that baseball should be included in the Olympic programme, while Peter Ueberroth, who was head of the 1984 Los Angeles Olympic organising committee and is now Commissioner of Major League Baseball, has been an effective international advocate for the game.

In most of the eighty or so countries that currently play baseball, the sport is controlled and operated entirely by an amateur federation. However, in the USA, Canada, Japan, South Korea, Mexico, Venezuela, Puerto Rico, Colombia and the Dominican Republic there are also professional baseball clubs, or a separate professional baseball organisation.

Amateur baseball in the USA is organised by a number of national, regional, state and local bodies, and has become the blueprint for many countries developing the sport. Some bodies operate only one age group on a regulation size field (e.g. American Legion Baseball), while others provide a number of age groups using smaller fields (e.g. PONY Baseball with six age groups ranging from seven to twenty years old). Most bodies use regulation baseball rules but also include special eligibility and safety requirements where appropriate.

The 19 million or so amateur baseball players in the USA have the opportunity to progress from about the age of five through a variety of programmes. The best amateurs may be selected to represent the USA under the auspices of the USBF. This may be for the junior team (sixteen to eighteen years old), or the senior side which plays in the Pan-American Games, the biennial World Championships, and invitation tournaments such as the Inter-Continental Cup. Each summer the USBF also plays two, best of seven games, fixtures against college students from Japan and South Korea.

The standard of college baseball in the USA is improving rapidly. More youngsters now prefer to gain college qualifications before trying their hand in the major leagues, and over two-thirds of today's major leaguers played in college. However, for some, the signing-on fee is too large to ignore. Star batter and outfielder Darryl Strawberry was set to attend Oklahoma State University, until the New York Mets offered him $280,000. Since the early 1960s the professional game in North America has seen expansion at the highest level, while the extensive grass-roots system of minor leagues has been radically re-organised, due to changes in population distribution across the USA and to economic constraints.

The USA's northern neighbour, Canada, has a strong amateur baseball programme at junior and senior levels, but few Canadians go on to play in the professional major leagues. This may change now that two professional franchises at Montreal and Toronto have established strong teams.

Between 1982 and 1984, about 50 players from thirteen countries other than the USA made their major league débuts. Most new major leaguers become national heroes in their own countries where their progress is followed closely by the media. The countries of Latin America are particularly proud of their major leaguers, who represent their baseball at the highest level.

Amateur baseball was introduced to Nicaragua in the early years of this century by US Marines. Today it is the national sport, and whatever players may lack due to shortages created by the civil war, they make up for in their enthusiasm for baseball, which seems to cut across political lines. There are about 80 players in the major leagues from Nicaragua and other Latin American countries such as Venezuela, Colombia and, particularly, Puerto Rico and the Dominican Republic. These have all had strong amateur baseball programmes for many years, and several have won the World Championships. The rich source of talent they offer is tapped by American managers, scouts, and players who play winter ball in Caribbean countries.

The supply of excellent Cuban-born players to the major leagues has all but dried up since the communist takeover of 1959. Cuba has concentrated on its already strong amateur baseball programme, winning the World Championship several times, and has found the game an excellent way of extending its influence in Latin America and beyond.

While all those countries play baseball for only part of the year, Mexico has both winter and summer leagues. This congested programme and local regulations mean that only ten Mexicans are currently playing in the majors. However, the success of Los Angeles Dodgers' pitcher Fernando Valenzuela, allied to Mexico's massive financial problems, has put clubs under increasing pressure to release their stars to play in the north.

The phenomenon of baseball's massive success in the Far East in the past century is worthy of a book in itself. Japan, Taiwan, South Korea and the Philippines have added an oriental flavour to the growing international diversity of baseball.

Baseball is South Korea's greatest spectator sport. Their professional league and high school championships series are played to a fine standard, while their national college team plays annually against the USA. Baseball's demonstration tournament at the 1988 Olympic Games will be played in the new 50,000-seat Jasmil Baseball Stadium at the centre of the Olympic complex in Seoul.

Taiwan has one of the best amateur teams in the world and an excellent record in children's baseball. Seven of their teams have won the Little League World Series ten times since 1969.

Amateur baseball was introduced to Japan in 1873 and became the major school sport from about the turn of the century. Japanese high schools have had two annual championships, one in Spring the other in Summer, for over 60 years. The university and college baseball championships were a major spectator sport until the Second World War, and still draw an entry of about 250 colleges, and massive media attention. Over 12½ million men, women and children play baseball in local parks with most using the hollow, soft, rubber baseball invented over 65 years ago. The pressure on facilities is so great that many Japanese play in the early morning, or at night under floodlights.

Visits from professional US All-Star teams of the highest quality before the Second World War helped the development of the Japanese game. The first professional team was formed after the 1934 visit, but it was not until 1950 that the professional game overtook amateur baseball as the major spectator attraction. Nowadays the two professional leagues, with six teams in each, play 130 games in a season that lasts from April to October, ending with the best of seven games 'Japan Series' (the equivalent of the North American 'World Series'). The Manchester United of Japanese baseball is the Yomiuri Giants who draw an average crowd of over 45,000.

The best Japanese players make little effort to seek their fortune in the North American major leagues, but over 200 American players have played in Japan since the war. However, all suffer problems adjusting to the deep cultural differences, Japanese attitudes to the game of baseball, and their perception of the foreigner, or 'gaijin', in it. Americans find Japanese Spring training camps a particularly gruelling round of conditioning, batting and fielding practice, meditation and massage.

Although Japanese clubs are keen to have one or two 'gaijin' players, each foreigner must subscribe to the 'wa' ethic if he is to retain his place in the side. The American player is expected to contribute to the club's success, but not become too successful himself, as that would be resented by team mates and opponents alike. The tacit understanding is that every player should be dedicated to the team at the expense of personal glory or reward. Few American players are able to come to terms with such a concept. Apart from the annual competition between US and Japanese college teams, and Spring training visits to the West Coast by Japanese clubs, many major league teams have made post-season exhibition tours to Japan, and all are finding it increasingly difficult to return home with a winning record.

In Europe, the strongest and best-organised amateur baseball is played in The Netherlands. There are four age-group leagues for youngsters from six to seventeen. Each of the nine Dutch districts organise their own adult leagues, and above this are the 66 teams in the four graded national leagues. The national championship has been played every year since 1922, and in 1985 The Netherlands won the European title for the twelfth time, beating their traditional rivals, Italy.

The Dutch have introduced baseball to countries such as The Netherlands Antilles and have always had strong links with South Africa, where the standard of baseball is as high as any played in Europe. Since the Second World War Dutch migrants have also contributed to the improving standard of baseball in Australia, where it used to be played mainly by cricketers in the winter months. For many years before the war baseball games were curtain raisers for Australian Rules Football matches in the VFL competition in Melbourne and Geelong, but the game has progressed since those days, and in recent years Australia's amateur baseball teams have excelled in the Junior and Senior World Championships and Inter-Continental Cup.

Amateur baseball is now played in at least 85 countries from all six continents. If soccer is the world's winter game, then baseball is fast becoming its summer equivalent.

CHAPTER SEVEN

BASEBALL IN BRITAIN

Although baseball's fortunes declined in Britain after the Second World War, the sport continued to be played in its traditional strongholds – the North-East, North-West, East Midlands and London. But in the last decade baseball has made notable advances in areas where it had no previous support, and is now gaining rapidly in popularity throughout the country.

How Baseball is Organised in Britain

The governing body of amateur baseball and softball in Britain is the British Amateur Baseball and Softball Federation (BABSF), which is affiliated to the International Baseball Association (IBA), the Confederation European Baseball Association (CEBA), and recognised by the Sports Council, the Central Council of Physical Recreation, and the British Olympic Association.

At present the strongest senior baseball leagues in Britain are in Greater London and the South-East (over 30 teams), Merseyside (eight teams), Humberside (eight teams), the North-East (six teams), and Nottingham (six teams). There are also three senior clubs in the West Midlands and one in the South-West. These teams usually play their local fixtures on Sunday afternoons. As some clubs only play teams from other regions in national cup competitions, the BABSF is hoping to improve standards by forming a National League. The few schools that currently play baseball as part of the curriculum tend to be concentrated in Essex, Humberside and Merseyside. Consequently, most youngsters who wish to play the game have to rely on local coaches giving instructional clinics during half-terms and holidays, or once or twice a week during term time. Those between seven and sixteen who become organised on a competitive basis usually play PONY League (UK) baseball matches on Saturday afternoons. The name PONY, incidentally, has no animal connection apart from the organisation's logo: the league was founded in the USA and its name is an acronym for Protect Our Nation's Youth.

Mindful of the need to have properly trained coaches, the BABSF started a coaching scheme in 1980 for senior baseball. Candidates take theory, oral and practical examinations to become qualified as a Teacher who may introduce baseball skills to beginners, or a Coach who may coach a club team. After at least five years' experience as a club coach a candidate may become a Senior Coach. The National Coaching Director and National Schools and Youth Officer are working towards making these senior awards continuous with the two junior training schemes for Youth Leader and Field Director.

Joining or Forming a Baseball Club

A stated priority of the BABSF is to give guidance and help over problems surrounding the formation of new baseball teams in the UK. All general enquiries for up-to-date information about baseball and softball should be made to the BABSF's headquarters in Hull. Those keen to start playing, coaching or umpiring baseball in the UK should contact their nearest Sports Council officer for the name and address of the BABSF officer for that region who will be able to help locally. Youngsters under the age of sixteen should also contact the National Schools and Youth Officer in Nottingham. A list of useful addresses is given at the end of the book.

The Sports Council has had a programme of grant aid designed to encourage and increase participation in sport in each of its nine regions. An example of the practicality of these regional participation grants for baseball was given in October 1984 when the Northern Region of the Sports Council and Gateshead MBC (which provided the administration, publicity and funding) staged, in co-ordination with the BABSF regional representative, a highly successful 'Demonstration-Come and Try It' event at Gateshead International Stadium. The success of the venture led to the formation of a Northern Baseball and Softball Association which started league fixtures in 1985, and was given a starter grant and assistance for two clubs to buy playing equipment.

Buying Baseball Equipment

Initially, players may prefer to learn the rudiments of the game using a soft tennis ball and the minimum of baseball equipment. Those who remain content to play baseball on lazy summer evenings in the park might only need to purchase a fielder's glove, which cost from about £25. A serviceable aluminium bat would cost about the same, although the latest graphite bats (which sound just like a wooden bat when they hit the ball) may retail at over £80. Those who catch 'baseball fever' and are keen to form a team to play in a local league, would need to invest in some of the club and individual playing equipment mentioned earlier in the book.

A new club could easily spend £500 on getting itself equipped to play league fixtures, while individual players would need a club uniform and cap, appropriate footwear, and a fielding glove. At the end of this guide there is a short list of sports shops able to supply baseball equipment. The list is by no means exhaustive, as many other sports shops will order items from wholesalers, or have an account with major American sports goods manufacturers which also produce baseball equipment.

CHAPTER EIGHT

BASEBALL RULES AND TERMS

To get the most from the game, every player, coach and fan should have an up-to-date copy of the Rules of Baseball and know it thoroughly. The most recent edition has about 100 pages of closely written text and almost every statement is accompanied by casebook examples, explanations, interpretations or exceptions. Consequently, it would be impractical here to do more than outline the more commonly encountered or unusual rules of the game not already mentioned in the book, and provide brief explanations for a few terms used by commentators on radio and television.

SOME BASEBALL RULES

Starting a game

The game begins when the first batter in the visiting team has taken his position in a batter's box, and the home team's starting pitcher stands with the ball in his hand and one foot on the pitcher's rubber. The home plate umpire then calls, 'Play', or 'Play Ball'.

The catcher must stay in his box behind home plate until the pitcher has pitched but the remaining seven fielders may stand wherever they wish as long as they are in fair territory. Players may change fielding positions with one another during the game but it is customary to tell the umpires when doing so.

Live and Dead Balls

Once the umpire calls 'Play' the ball is live and remains in play until the umpire declares it dead by calling 'Time'. An umpire cannot rule the ball dead until all action on a play has ended, even if a batter, fielder or runner has been injured. When the ball is dead, players on the batting side may not be put out, run bases or score runs. However, runners may advance as a result of acts when the ball was live, such as, a home run, a balk or interference.

The Infield Fly Rule

The infield fly rule prevents an infielder deliberately not catching the ball so that he can get a double play on the runners who are forced to remain close to their bases, in order to avoid being trapped off base when a fly ball is caught. The rule only applies when a fair fly ball is hit with less than two batters out, and when 1st and 2nd, or 1st, 2nd and 3rd bases are occupied, and for fly balls which the umpire judges could be caught by an infielder with normal effort. In a game situation the umpire will call 'Infield Fly' and the batter is automatically out. This means that base runners need not run if the ball is not caught, although they may do so. The rule does not apply if there is no runner on 1st base as no one is forced to move on. All this may seem unduly complicated, but the rule is necessary to stop fielders gaining an unfair advantage.

Use of Fielder's Equipment

A fielder may not use any of his equipment or uniform in an unsporting manner. For example, he cannot catch, stop or deflect any hit or thrown ball with his cap, or any item of his detached uniform (such as a catcher's mask), or hit it with his thrown glove. (However, there is no penalty if the thrown glove misses the ball.)

If a fielded ball becomes wedged in the webbing of the glove he may throw it, glove and ball, to another fielder to put the runner out.

The Batter

Once ready in the batter's box to receive a pitch, the batter may not crouch low to make his strike zone smaller in an attempt to gain a walk (base on balls). If the umpire suspects the batter's stance is exaggerated he should call the pitch a strike.

A batter is at liberty to hit any pitch (even if it first hits the ground and bounces towards the plate), but may not leave the batter's box to do so. A batter may be replaced by a pinch-hitter during his time at bat, but the count against him (e.g. one ball and two strikes) is not erased but passed on to the pinch-hitter.

There are more than a dozen ways in which a batter may be out. Two of the less obvious are when a batter bunts the ball foul on a 3rd strike, and if he attempts to hit a 3rd strike, but the ball hits him. (Unlike in cricket, a baseball batter's hands are not counted as part of the bat.)

The Base Runner

A base runner is out if he passes any preceding runner or, to avoid being tagged, he runs more than three feet away from a direct line between bases, unless he is avoiding a fielder fielding a batted ball. He is also out if he intentionally interferes with a thrown ball or hinders a fielder attempting to make a play on a batted ball unless the runner is in contact with a legally occupied base. He is not out if accidentally hit or 'plugged' by a thrown ball.

If, during a play, a base is knocked loose from its proper place by a runner he cannot be tagged out there. Any following runner only has to touch or occupy the space where the base should have been to be safe.

A Balk

A balk is an illegal motion by a pitcher when one or more runners are on base. If a balk is called by an umpire each base runner advances one base, although the batter is not awarded 1st base. If no runners are on base then the umpire will call a ball instead for each balk offence committed.

There are many circumstances under which a balk may be committed, but the two most commonly called in the major leagues are:
a) when a pitcher who is touching the pitcher's rubber does not step towards a base before throwing to it
b) when he delivers a pitch from the set position without coming to a stop.

A Relief Pitcher

When a relief pitcher is brought into the game to replace the starting pitcher he is normally allowed a minute in which to throw a few warm-up pitches. The relief pitcher must then pitch until one batter is retired, reaches a base or the side is retired, before he in turn may be replaced.

A Run

A run is scored each time a base runner touches 1st, 2nd, 3rd base and home plate safely before three players on his team are put out to end the inning. An exception occurs when a runner advances to home plate when the 3rd out of the inning is:

a) the batter-runner before he is able to touch 1st base,

b) any runner who is forced out, or,

c) a preceding runner declared out because he failed to touch a base.

COMMON BASEBALL TERMS

Aboard: Waiting on base. One, two or three runners may be aboard.

Appeal: A claim by a fielder for a rules violation which is not automatically penalised.

Around the horn: Throws relayed the longest way round the infield, from 3rd, to 2nd, to 1st base. The term derives from the Cape Horn route from the East to the West coast of the USA.

Assist: A throw to a fellow fielder enabling him to make a put out.

Automatic take: A pitch thrown when the count is three balls and no strikes. The batter does not swing at the pitch, hoping it will be called ball four and he will be awarded 1st base.

Bail out: When a batter falls away to avoid being hit by a pitch.

Balk: An illegal action by a pitcher when at least one runner is on base.

Ball: A pitch which does not enter the strike zone in flight and is not struck at by the batter (see Base on balls).

Base on balls: 1st base is awarded to a batter after receiving four balls in his turn at bat.

Bases loaded: 1st, 2nd and 3rd bases all occupied by runners.

Bat around: When a team's nine batters bat in one inning before three are out.

Beanball: An illegal pitch thrown at a batter's head. The pitcher would claim he had merely thrown a Brushback.

Beat out: When a batter hits safely, beating a fielder's throw to a base.

Between the lines: Fair territory between the right and left foul lines.

Bleeder: A lucky hit that trickles through the infield. Also called a 'squib', 'nubber', or 'scratch hit'.

Bottom: The last, or lower half of an inning when the home team is at bat.

Breaking ball Any moving pitch such as a curve, slider, knuckleball, or screwball.

Brushback: A pitch thrown high to the inside of the strike zone which causes the batter to move backwards. A 'duster'.

Bunt: When a batter allows a pitch to hit a dead bat, so that the ball only rolls a few feet into the infield.

Called game: A game ended early for any reason by the umpire-in-chief. (e.g. for rain or darkness.)

Catcher's interference: If impeded by the catcher, a batter is awarded 1st base.

Chance: An opportunity to catch or field a batted ball.

Change-up: Any slower pitch, usually thrown with the same action as a fast ball.

Choke: To hold the bat down the handle, or to fail under pressure.

Clutch: A clutch player succeeds when the team needs him most. A 'money player'.

Count: the number of balls and strikes a batter has received (e.g. two and one). A Full Count is three balls and two strikes.

Curve: A breaking pitch. Known variously as a 'hook', 'snake', or 'yakker'.

Cut-off man: He intercepts a throw from the outfield with the intention of stopping runners advancing.

Cycle: When a batter hits a single, double, triple, and home run in one game.

Dead ball: When the umpire declares the ball out of play, by calling 'Time'.

Double: A two-base hit.

Double play: A play in which two players are put out.

Drag bunt: A bunt that is pulled across the batter's body. A push bunt goes away from his body.

Duster: Similar to Beanball or Brushback depending on your point of view. Also called a 'purpose pitch'.

Earned run: When a pitcher is held accountable for a run that is scored. (E.R.A. means Earned Run Average).

Error: A clear, officially charged fielding mistake, fumble or wild throw.

Fielder's choice: When a fielder does not throw the ball to 1st base to retire the batter-runner, but chooses to throw to 2nd, 3rd, or home plate to retire a different runner.

Fly ball: A ball hit high in the air.

Forced out: When a fielder retires a base runner by touching the base to which the runner is forced to advance.

Foul ball: A batted ball that lands in foul territory, or rolls foul before reaching 1st or 3rd base.

Foul tip: A sharp, direct batted ball that goes backwards and is legally caught by the catcher.

Grand Slam: When a home run is hit with all three bases occupied by base runners. Four runs are scored.

Ground out: When a batter hits a grounder to a fielder who then throws to 1st base for the put out.

Ground rules: Special rules to make allowances for known peculiarities or obstructions. (e.g. only a double if a fair hit ball bounces over the outfield fence.)

Grounder: A batted ball that rolls or bounces along the ground.

Home Run: When a batter hits the ball and completes a circuit touching all three bases and back to home plate without stopping. Also known as a 'homer', 'tater', 'round tripper', or 'dinger'.

Hop: A term used to describe the bounce of the ball. Hence, from the fielder's point of view, a 'good hop' or a 'bad hop'.

Inning: A half-inning is when a team takes its turn at bat. An inning is completed when both teams have batted once.

Line drive: A hard hit ball on a low straight course. Known also as a 'screamer' or 'frozen rope'.

Losing pitcher: Usually the pitcher who is relieved when his team is trailing and does not recover to tie the score.

No hitter: When no base hits and no runs are conceded by a pitcher throughout a game. (See Perfect game.)

Out in order: When a pitcher retires the first three batters in an inning.

Overslide: When a base runner slides into 2nd, 3rd, or home plate but loses contact with the base, so risks being put out.

Passed ball: Charged against a catcher who fails to gather a pitch he should have controlled, and enables a runner to advance.

Perfect game: A no-hitter where only 27 batters are faced by a pitcher in 9 innings and not one reaches base.

Pick off: To catch a base runner off base with a throw.

Pick up: A ball collected by a fielder on the half-volley, straight after it hits the ground.

Pinch hitter: A player who is substituted to bat in place of another hitter, and is then removed from the game before he has a chance to field.

Pinch runner: A fast runner who is substituted for a slower player (who has reached a base safely), and is subseqently removed himself.

Pitch: A ball delivered to the batter by the pitcher.

Pitchout: A pitch thrown deliberately wide of the plate to the catcher when a runner is attempting to steal.

Pivot foot: A pitcher's pivot foot must be in contact with the pitcher's plate (rubber) when delivering the ball.

Pop fly: A ball hit high and caught in the infield. Also referred to as a 'pop up'.

Power alleys: The spaces between outfielders. Hits up the alleys are called 'tweeners'.

Pull hitter: A player who hits the ball across his body towards the foul line.

Putout: When a player is retired by a fielder.

R.B.I.: A run batted in, or 'ribby', is usually credited for each run scored because of an offensive action by a batter.

Rundown: An attempt to put out a runner caught between bases.

Runner: An offensive player who is approaching, touching or returning to any base.

Sandlot: An informal game of baseball, usually played by youngsters on whatever ground is available.

Save: This is credited to a relief pitcher who finishes a game, and protects a lead for the winning pitcher for a least three innings. (A winning pitcher must pitch at least five innings.)

Screwball: A pitch with the opposite break to a curveball. Also known as a 'scroogie'.

Single: A base hit when only lst base is reached safely by the batter.

Smoke: When a pitcher is throwing particularly fiercely and fast.

Spray hitter: A batter who is able to hit to all parts of the field.

Strike out: When a batter is out charged with three strikes.

Swinging bunt: Used to describe when a batter makes a full swing at a pitch but only succeeds in hitting the ball gently a few feet into the infield, as if it was a bunt.

Tag: A tag occurs when a fielder, holding the ball in his hand or glove, touches a base with his body, or touches a runner with his hand or the glove which is holding the ball.

Triple: A three-base hit, or 'three bagger'.

Unearned run: The result of an error, passed ball, or interference.

Wild Pitch: A poorly directed pitch that is not handled successfully by the catcher, and which allows a base runner to advance.

USEFUL ADDRESSES

Baseball Organisations

Professional Major League Baseball:
Commissioner Peter V. Ueberroth, 350 Park Avenue, New York, New York 10022, USA.

International (Amateur) Baseball Association:
President Dr Robert Smith, 315 East College Avenue, Greenville College, Greenville, Illinois 62246, USA.

British Amateur Baseball and Softball Federation:
BABSF Headquarters, (President Mr Don Smallwood), 197 Newbridge Road, Hull, HU9 2LR Humberside. (Telephone: 0482-76169).

Local BABSF officers may be contacted through these Sports Council offices:
1. Northern Region: County Court Building, Hallgarth Street, Durham DH1 3PB. (Northumberland, Cumbria, Durham, Cleveland, Tyne & Wear)
2. Yorkshire and Humberside: Coronet House, Queen Street, Leeds LS1 4PW. (N. Yorks, W Yorks, S. Yorks, Humberside)
3. North West: Byrom House, Quay Street, Manchester M3 5FJ. (Lancs, Cheshire, Gr. Manchester, Merseyside).
4. East Midlands: 26 Musters Road, West Bridgford, Nottingham NG2 7PL. (Derbyshire, Notts, Lincs, Leics, Northants)
5. West Midlands: Metropolitan House, 1 Hagley Road, Five Ways,

Birmingham B16 8TT. (Hereford & Worcester, Salop, Staffs, Warwickshire, West Midlands)
6. Eastern: 26-28 Bromham Road, Bedford MK40 2QD. (Norfolk, Cambs, Suffolk, Beds, Herts, Essex)
7. Gr. London & South East: 160 Great Portland Street, London W1N 5TB. (Gr. London, Surrey, Kent, E.Sussex, W. Sussex)
8. Southern: Watlington House, Watlington Street, Reading, Berkshire RG1 4RJ. (Hampshire, Isle of Wight, Berks, Bucks, Oxfordshire)
9. South Western: Ashlands House, Ashlands, Crewkerne, Somerset TA18 7LQ (Avon, Cornwall, Devon, Dorset, Somerset, Wiltshire, Gloucestershire)

The headquarters of the **Sports Council** are at 16 Upper Woburn Place, London WC1 H OQP. (01-388-1277)

BABSF National Schools and Youth Officer:
Mr Benny Benson, 82 Manesty Crescent, Clifton Estate, Nottingham NG 11 9DU.

Suppliers of Baseball Equipment

Surfside & Alpine Sports Centre, 714 Mansfield Road, Nottingham. (Can supply many famous makes of equipment)
George H. Crawford, 166 Holderness Road, Hull, North Humberside HU9 2AG. (Rawlings, Wilson, Cooper)
Freetime Sports Ltd, 2 Old Market Place, Grimsby, South Humberside DN31 1DT. (Can order most items)
Viscount Sports, Nook Lane, Latchford, Warrington, Cheshire WA4 1NQ. (Hillerich & Bradsby)
Hawkinsport Ltd, 51 Friars Square, Aylesbury, Bucks HP20 2TA.
Gridiron Sports, 59 Walham Grove, Fulham, London SW6. (MacGregor, Rawlings, Wilson)
Slick Willies, 47 Kensington High Street, London W8. (Can supply most famous brands)

Illustration Acknowledgement. The publishers wish to thank Technical Art Services for creating the diagrams, and Jerry Malone for the illustrations which appear in this book.